Praise for *Brilliant Su*

'Positive, engaging and motivational … the personal tone and examples of success stories make the content seem realistic and achievable. I see this book on many teachers' bookshelves and staffroom resource lists!'

Amanda Anker, classroom teacher

'As a teacher who continually struggles to achieve the ideal work–life balance and is relatively new to subject leadership, this book helped to demystify the role of a subject leader and provides brilliant tips and timesavers which are proving to be invaluable resources.'

Sally Bunyan, subject leader

'Marc expertly manages to combine a clear, concise and informative guide to subject leadership with personal accounts from his own real-life experiences which add meaning, a sense of empathy and humour!

A truly engaging and motivational book. A must-have for every school.'

Sarah Volante, subject leader

brilliant

subject
leader

brilliant

subject
leader

What you need to know to be a truly outstanding teacher

Marc Bowen

Prentice Hall
is an imprint of

Harlow, England • London • New York • Boston • San Francisco • Toronto • Sydney • Singapore • Hong Kong
Tokyo • Seoul • Taipei • New Delhi • Cape Town • Madrid • Mexico City • Amsterdam • Munich • Paris • Milan

PEARSON EDUCATION LIMITED

Edinburgh Gate
Harlow CM20 2JE
Tel: +44 (0)1279 623623
Fax: +44 (0)1279 431059
Website: www.pearsoned.co.uk

First published in Great Britain in 2011

Pearson Education is not responsible for the content of third party internet sites.

ISBN: 978-0-273-73248-8

British Library Cataloguing-in-Publication Data
A catalogue record for this book is available from the British Library

Library of Congress Cataloging-in-Publication Data
Bowen, Marc.
  Brilliant subject leader : what you need to know to be a truly outstanding teacher / Marc Bowen.
    p. cm.
  Includes index.
  ISBN 978-0-273-73248-8 (pbk.)
  1. Curriculum evaluation–Great Britain. 2. Curriculum planning–Great Britain. 3. Teacher participation in administration–Great Britain. 4. Effective teaching. I. Title.
  LB1570.B73 2011
  375'.006–dc22
                              2010050031

10 9 8 7 6 5 4 3 2 1
15 14 13 12 11

Typeset in 10/14pt Plantin by 3
Printed by Ashford Colour Press Ltd, Gosport

For Rich, Adrian, Gaynor, Natalie and the 'two Nancys' for their infinite support and guidance.

Contents

About the author

Marc Bowen was born and raised in the Welsh Valleys, developing an early desire to work in education, as a result of his inspirational primary school teachers. After completing his secondary schooling at a local comprehensive, he moved to Bath to study a combined education and English degree course. Graduating in 2000, Marc started work in a small village primary school, where he was thrown into the role of improving the ICT capacity of the school, despite being a newly qualified teacher. During this time, his enthusiasm for teaching and ability to strategically develop ICT was recognised by local authority advisors, who arranged a weekly secondment to another school to support their ICT development. It was here that Marc was headhunted by the headteacher of another local school and, in this new post, led the school to achieve a number of ICT awards from national bodies and educational institutions, as well as developing a new, comprehensive structure for subject leadership across the school – a model which was adopted by many other local schools.

Marc has subsequently worked with the Qualifications and Curriculum Authority on the Futures Curriculum project, supported the development of national pupil voice materials, presented at national seminars and collaborated with other schools to develop their approaches to a creative curriculum. Marc is currently leading on ICT, Assessment and Leadership Succession as deputy head at a school in Wiltshire and enjoys writing for educational publications in his spare time.

Acknowledgements

I would like to thank Anne Orme for opening my eyes to the world of subject leadership and providing numerous opportunities for my own leadership development.

I would also like to thank the many dedicated and outstanding colleagues who have been part of my journey through the role of the subject leader, especially those who have challenged my thinking and helped to reduce my impact on the world's rainforests.

A big thank you to all the staff and children at Colerne CE Primary School who have all, in some way, influenced my own professional practice.

Finally, sincere thanks to Rich for tolerating my need to be locked away in the writing den, with only *Brilliant Subject Leader* for company.

Foreword

I began my teaching career in 1976 and was quick to achieve promotion to a Scale 2 post with responsibility for Art and Craft. The more mature readers of this book will remember the system and know that a small additional amount was put into my pay packet on the understanding that I kept the art materials tidy and occasionally came up with advice on how to achieve a tie-dyed effect without splattering the classroom walls and floors with Brusho and incurring the wrath of the caretaker! Some colleagues at the time had similar allowances for keeping cupboards tidy, running the staff tea fund or organising sports day. How times have changed – and quite rightly so!

An effective modern school must deliver a vibrant, broad curriculum capable of responding to the needs of the local community. All members of staff play their part in this delivery but nobody more so than the subject leaders who must provide both professional leadership and management of their subject/s. Subject leaders must support and challenge their colleagues to ensure effective curriculum provision that will result in improving standards of learning and achievement for all pupils. Many young teachers will find themselves having to support far more experienced colleagues who may, or may not, appreciate the support. This requires sensitivity and can be daunting!

When I first met Marc I was instantly impressed by his subject knowledge, but what impressed me even more was his ability to gently support and encourage – often resistant – colleagues until they too shared his passion for the subject. His organisational abilities are second to none and he uses this strength to great effect in his managerial role. Above all, he has an empathy with colleagues across the range of ability and confidence levels found in any school and is able to offer support and/or challenge to suit individual circumstances. Marc is a natural teacher and is never happier than when in front of a class. He has the respect of all who know or work with him and I can think of no better person to write this book.

The prospect of becoming a subject leader can be extremely daunting. However, this book will provide an invaluable resource for both new and experienced subject leaders. With its sound, practical advice and no-nonsense approach it will enable readers to dip in and out at will to find support to enable them to develop their important and influential role within the school. The easy-to-read format includes Brilliant dos and don'ts, Brilliant tips, Brilliant timesavers and Brilliant examples which together provide not only a practical survival guide, but reassurance to those who doubt their role or their ability to fulfil it. Within the pages of this book, subject leaders will find encouragement and inspiration to improve their effectiveness within the school. At the end of each chapter there is a Brilliant recap that succinctly provides the key messages in an easily digested format for subject leaders under pressure. Despite the dip in and out format, this book deserves to be read in its entirety: it is a good read and places a great emphasis on working smarter, not harder, to achieve a healthy work–life balance and greater job satisfaction.

Marc refers to subject leaders as the unsung heroes of the school: with the help of this superb guide they may well remain unsung heroes, but they will be Brilliant Subject Leaders!

Mrs Anne Orme
Retired headteacher and National Teaching Awards winner 2008

Introduction

Over recent years there has been a quiet but significant evolution in the role of the subject leader, reflecting the current national focus on school self-evaluation and the effectiveness of school leadership at all levels of an institution. The core purpose of a subject leader is to be the individual who can provide professional leadership and management of their subject/s, supporting and challenging colleagues to ensure that curriculum provision is effective in improving standards of learning and achievement for all pupils.

Until the publication of the National Standards for Subject Leaders in 1998 by the TDA (then the Teacher Training Agency), there had been no agreed national guidance for this specific role which led to great variation in the effectiveness of subject leaders. Prior to this, the title of 'subject coordinator' was predominantly used, which resulted in many interpreting the role as being simply managerial: auditing resources, ensuring the effective organisation of teaching materials and essentially making sure that the subject 'happened' in the school. The effectiveness of the subject did not always feature as a key aspect of the coordinator's role.

The advent of the National Standards for Subject Leaders resulted in an uneasy transition for many professionals, who had previously been comfortable with the practicalities of subject coordination but were now also expected to evaluate the impact of their subject across the school and to ensure improvement and high standards. In essence, not all subject coordinators wanted to get out of the cupboard and take a look at the quality of their subject in the cold light of day. However, we must now acknowledge that subject leaders are accountable for the achievement and standards within their area of curriculum responsibility and have a vital role in ensuring the overall effectiveness of the school.

For many teachers who are at an early stage of their career, the prospect of becoming a subject leader can be extremely daunting. The professional development received by new teachers, as part of their initial teacher training, in preparation for their role as subject leaders varies greatly and therefore the responsibility for this essential training often falls to the individual and the school within which they work.

As a new subject leader, the National Standards can be an overwhelming and confusing read. Fundamentally, an effective subject leader should aim to:

- strategically lead their subject with consideration for whole school priorities, targets, policies and the specific context of the school;
- ensure curriculum provision, including resources, is effective and has a positive impact on achievement and standards;
- support and challenge colleagues, where necessary, to meet the high expectations of the subject;
- make effective use of pupil tracking data to secure high standards;
- maintain a good understanding of their subject, including current educational thinking and national agendas;
- work in support of and in collaboration with the local community, including parents, as well as seeking out opportunities to enhance learning through national and international links.

This book is intended to help subject leaders, especially those new to the role, to gain a clearer understanding of how to be effective in their leadership role and to balance this against the demands of class teaching responsibilities and the vibrant but busy daily life of schools. It is also important to remember that, as well as being teachers and subject leaders, we professionals are individuals with lives outside the school building. In this sense, being an effective subject leader is also about being able to protect that precious free time to ensure we are also effective human beings!

Before exploring specific elements of the subject leader's role in detail, it is important to acknowledge that the common language of school self-evaluation can sometimes be misunderstood and misused. There are three basic principles that need clarification in the minds of all professionals seeking to evaluate, lead and improve a subject.

1   Teaching and learning are linked but must also be examined as distinct entities. They influence each other but have unique and important aspects, which will be explored in more depth in Chapter 3.

2   Monitoring and evaluation are often spoken in the same breath. They are different. Monitoring is essentially developing an evidence base, whereas evaluation is the interrogation of this evidence resulting in positive action.

3   The question of 'So what?' Whilst this is reminiscent of a difficult teenager's rant, it is actually a good question to ask whenever a subject leader is making observations, judgements or strategic decisions. Basically, how has what you have seen, done or intend to do impacted upon teaching, learning and standards? The answers can often help to refine decision making and distil the correct course of action.

The following chapters are intended to help subject leaders in their role, highlighting the professional skills and attributes that can make us all more effective in our leadership roles. However, it is important to remember that as already busy teachers who want to have a realistic work–life balance, we should be *working smarter, not harder* as subject leaders by becoming Brilliant Subject Leaders!

CHAPTER 1

Why become a
subject leader?

I f you ask a teacher to share what inspired them to join the profession, you will commonly hear stories of vibrant teachers from childhood, treasured memories of exciting learning experiences or moments which switched on the learning light bulb in a young mind. I would challenge you to find a colleague who committed considerable time and effort to train as a teacher because of the outstanding monitoring and evaluation by a subject leader! The best teachers are driven by a desire to provide valuable and enriching learning experiences for their pupils; an inexhaustible enthusiasm for working with children and helping them to excel which emanates from the teacher and permeates everything they do. It is this that many children respond to and which will motivate some to become teachers themselves.

Why then would we, as child-centred, learning-focused teachers, wish to take on a subject leadership role with duties and responsibilities that are often one or more steps removed from our 'chalk-face' work in the classroom? The answer is simple: because we genuinely care about the education and wellbeing of children.

brilliant tip

It is easy to feel swamped by an endless array of tasks that you could do as a subject leader, and trying to fulfil them all might

▶

result in you being very busy at achieving nothing. To help you prioritise your valuable time, keep this simple question in mind: 'Will this task have a positive impact on the children in our school?' If the answer to this is *no*, then is it worth doing?

As class teachers, we all have the potential to exert positive influences over our learners, devising meaningful and well-pitched sequences of lessons which meet the academic needs of those in our care. We are also able to build strong pastoral relationships with the children in our classes, sometimes helping to coach them through difficult personal challenges. Though these relationships and experiences often have a powerful impact on the children we encounter, their effectiveness is limited to the children we teach. In your classroom role, you may teach one single class for a whole academic year or you may only see one select group within a cohort on a weekly basis. What about the rest of the children in the school?

It is at a whole school level that a subject leader can extend the scope of their influence and spread their expertise more broadly for the benefit of a wider range of pupils in the school. As a class teacher, you are able to monitor the effectiveness of your teaching, build on successes and respond to the inevitable 'bad days' with a positive 'can-do' attitude. However, as a subject leader you will be instrumental in ensuring that all colleagues are providing the right level of learning for their pupils. It is you that will be supporting colleagues to develop their practice which will result in effective classroom learning and it will be your responsibility to ensure that the most relevant and useful resources are available to support enhanced learning experiences. You will be the person that leads a subject which will be enjoyed by all the children in the school, irrespective of age, cohort or timetable arrangements. If you are an effective subject leader, you will proactively develop, monitor and evaluate effective teaching and ultimately secure the best learning opportunities for the pupils in the school.

An integral role

We can think of subject leaders as often being the unsung heroes of the school; the individuals that work behind the scenes, analogous with backstage workers in the world of theatre. Subject leaders help to prepare the teachers for their performance in the classroom. They are also the directors and producers of the school curriculum, ensuring that learning is effectively structured into acts and scenes which make sense to their young audience; they are the stage hands who source and gather the props to augment the theatre of the classroom; and they are the prompters waiting in the wings to provide that all important support when their performers are in need. On occasion, they also need to be the (supportive) critic who holds up a mirror to the quality of a teacher's performance.

> we can think of subject leaders as the unsung heroes of the school

Whilst the children we teach during our careers may not look back on our time spent tracking assessment data, auditing resources or monitoring learning with fond memories, they will feel the warmth of support, care and guidance they received long into adulthood because of our determination and diligence in securing the best teaching and learning in our schools.

Career progression

Throughout this book, the intention is to check the balance between you as a professional with a commitment to your school and you as an individual with a commitment to a healthy, enjoyable and rewarding life. It is therefore important to also consider the challenges and benefits of subject leadership for you as an individual before taking on the role.

experiences gained as a subject leader can help to shape the school leaders of the future

For many, becoming a subject leader is the first step onto the leadership ladder. Whilst senior school leadership and ultimately headship might seem a distant goal for some at this point, or even a step too far for others, it is the experiences gained as a subject leader which can help to shape the school leaders of the future. It is true that for the majority of your time as a subject leader you will be involved in a cycle of curriculum monitoring, evaluation and development which will have been standardised by your school or local authority. However, for those who wish to progress further as school leaders, this first role can open many other doors.

 **brilliant** example

The accidental leader

As a newly qualified teacher, I had no desire to do anything else with my career but be the best teacher possible and to enjoy my experiences in the classroom. I was (and hopefully still am) child-centred and totally committed to making my classroom a hub of meaningful and memorable learning for the children in my class. The prospect of school leadership was a distant and frankly undesirable aspect of our profession and one which I had no aspirations to reach.

However, it was in my NQT year that I unwittingly started my journey through school leadership when I was given the role of ICT subject leader. With subsequent experience I am now aware that giving a subject leader role to an NQT is virtually unheard of nowadays, but at this time it was a necessity as I was working in a very small school and there was also the desperate need for ICT curriculum development. So, with my youthful and boundless enthusiasm for my new career, I naturally applied the same commitment and child-centred approach to subject leadership as I did in the classroom. I soon discovered, more by accident than by design, that this enthusiasm was infectious and within no time at all my previously ICT-phobic colleagues in the school were seeking out opportunities to make greater use of it in their teaching.

Without my knowledge, word of the contagion also spread to the local authority advisor for ICT, via my headteacher, and as a result I was asked to work on behalf of the local authority for one day a week in a local school which had recently been placed in special measures. In hindsight, I now understand that this was a significant leadership role in that I was the key individual being asked to lead and develop the whole team of teaching and non-teaching staff in their use of ICT. However, I was still simply applying the principles of good quality teaching and learning that I held dear in the classroom. I was communicating this to other professionals in a positive and enthusiastic manner, whilst also responding to their individual needs, attitudes and previous experiences. Again, the skills of a good teacher were being upscaled for use with colleagues.

Having engendered a growing enthusiasm for ICT at this school, my journey as an accidental leader continued when I was asked to speak at a number of local and national ICT conferences. In my mind, I was merely providing a mildly interesting sideshow at these conferences, sandwiched between the educational big-hitters of school leadership. However, with each seminar and every post-presentation chat with colleagues I began to realise that people were looking to me as a leader. It was then that the definition of a school leader was clarified in my mind. They weren't necessarily people who emerged from the womb with a clipboard, data sheet and a snappy suit (although I have indeed met some members of that unique species in my time); they were in fact more often those colleagues who possessed an enthusiasm for teaching, learning and the broader aims of education for personal development and the empowerment of the individual to better themselves.

From this point, I was fortunate enough to encounter a truly inspirational headteacher in the form of Anne Orme. It was she who recognised my potential for school leadership, even when I couldn't see it myself,

▷

and helped me to more coherently plot my route into eventual senior school leadership. I can now appreciate that I underwent the necessary metamorphosis from the reluctant, accidental school leader to one who understood the power for change and positive influence that leaders at all levels can wield for the benefit of the pupils in their care.

Working as a subject leader within a school can provide you with the opportunity to flex your muscles as a school leader, without the weight of additional responsibility that may be associated with more senior positions such as heads of department, year group leaders or senior leadership. The role requires you to lead other staff from across the school, many of whom may be older and professionally more experienced than yourself. This can be a challenge in itself but equally can help your colleagues to view you in a more professional light as your leadership qualities begin to shine through.

your leadership qualities begin to shine through

brilliant dos and don'ts

If you are now considering taking on the adventure that is subject leadership, you may well have to interview for a post. Here are some helpful hints for that all important interview.

Do

✔ Know the subject: you haven't got to be a world expert but you must know the content of the curriculum, including age-appropriate expectations.

✔ Read around the subject: educational research is always taking place and many subjects have national associations. Take a look at their website or publications to ensure you are aware of the latest thinking.

✔ Find out about the subject in the school: if you are considering an internal application then use this to your advantage by discussing the subject and the priorities with existing staff, review the school development plan for any targets in the subject and, if possible, chat informally to the subject leader you plan to succeed. If you are applying externally, then make sure you visit the school and ask lots of questions to begin to build up your understanding. The interview panel won't expect you to know everything but they will be reassured by your proactive interest prior to the interview.

Don't

✘ Criticise the school's current approach to the subject: they may be appointing a new subject leader to implement change but negativity won't engender trust at this early stage. Instead, suggest some enhancements you might action.

✘ Try to cover up any gaps in your knowledge: interview panels will chase any discrepancies with further questions. Instead, be honest about your own development needs, sharing anything you are already doing to address these (for example, educational reading, training at your current school) and showing a willingness to engage with continuing professional development (CPD).

✘ Only refer to your experience of teaching the subject. If you are still early in your career, you may be applying for a subject that you have only taught to a single year group, or had limited experience of across the school. Try to avoid relying on this too heavily to exemplify any points you are making, as this may exaggerate your lack of broader experience to the rest of the panel. Instead, try to refer to your knowledge of other colleagues' work in the subject or even experiences gained through your initial teacher training. This will subtly show your understanding of the need to consider the subject at a whole school, rather than single class, level.

Subject leadership responsibilities can also herald opportunities to work beyond your school. In many areas, cluster groups of schools are establishing subject leader networks where colleagues are able to work on collaborative subject development, action research and exciting learning events in their area. For those looking to rapidly progress their careers, such cluster working can provide excellent insights into different forms of school leadership and the variety of leadership structures that have been developed, as well as helping to build networks in the local authority.

Ultimately, whether you have goals to be part of a future school leadership team or merely want the opportunity to develop your leadership skills beyond the classroom, subject leadership can be a valuable and worthwhile experience. Approach the role with the same child-centred and learning-focused manner that you adopt in the classroom, keep a positive work–life balance and you will reap the rewards of increased professional confidence and personal growth. In time, I hope that you too will feel as lucky and as privileged I do to be a subject leader.

 **brilliant** recap

The four most important messages from this chapter for the Brilliant Subject Leader are:

1   The role of the subject leader can offer excellent early leadership experience, without the pressure of senior school leadership.

2   As a subject leader, you will often gain more experience and observe good practice by working with counterpart colleagues in other schools and institutions; you can then use this experience to benefit your own school.

3   The role can be highly rewarding as you are scaling up your positive influence over the education of a larger group of pupils.

4   Remember to maintain a positive work–life balance: exhausting yourself in the classroom and burning the midnight oil as a subject leader will lead to you doing neither very well and not having a life! Be organised and partition your time to match the demands of your new role.

CHAPTER 2

Auditing your subject

As a subject leader there are a myriad of tasks, actions and activities you could be undertaking which would certainly occupy a lot of your time and would let colleagues see you being 'busy' in your leadership role. However, simply being 'busy' does not mean that you are being effective. To be truly effective you must know your subject well.

> to be truly effective you must know your subject well

Here we must make an important distinction. It is often wrongly assumed that the best subject leaders are those that possess some personal skill, talent or interest in the subject they lead. Does owning a tracksuit automatically make an individual an effective PE subject leader? Will a DIY enthusiast naturally raise standards in Design and Technology? The answer to both these questions is a resounding *no*! Knowing your subject is more about the contextualised reality of teaching and learning of the subject in your school, rather than knowing every abstract fact, figure and interesting tit-bit on the topic. There are those fortunate colleagues whose personal hobbies and interests tie in with the subject they lead, which can help to enhance the impact they have as a subject leader, and some secondary colleagues can choose to lead a subject that they specialise in, but in most primary schools we are often simply assigned a subject because of the necessity that each subject has an assigned leader. It is therefore essential that before we take any action in our roles, we must establish where the subject sits in terms of curriculum provision, teaching and learning. Once we have this information at our fingertips we can then implement actions and lead developments which will be effective in improving the learning experiences for the pupils in our schools.

Where are we now and where do we need to be?

This is the first question you should ask yourself. To a certain extent, the school leadership team, performance management leader or assessment leader may have already identified aspects of your subject which should be prioritised for development, as part of the school self-evaluation processes. For example, in the case of core subject areas, there may already be a huge amount of information available in the form of assessment analyses and pupil tracking which will clearly highlight some of the school's needs in your subject. Equally, performance management leaders may already be aware of the specific training needs of individuals within the school, linked to your subject. However, at this senior leadership level there will probably be little or no awareness of the specific needs of your subject beyond these headline issues. This is where the role of the subject leader is vital to the continuous development and improvement of a subject within a school.

one method of gathering information is to perform an audit

One method of gathering information about the foundations of your subject is to perform an audit. This term is often part of subject leader parlance but the power of this form of monitoring is not always fully understood. By performing an audit, you are essentially taking a snapshot of a specific aspect of your subject at a given time, in order to inform yourself about the possible priorities. Audits can be conducted for an endless array of purposes and can provide a useful insight, providing there is a clear purpose for doing so. We will look at some possible means of conducting audits for two popular topics: subject resources and colleagues' subject skills, knowledge and understanding.

Auditing subject resources

At the most basic level, a subject leader could audit the resources for their subject by going into the storage area, making a list of the available equipment and filing this away as proof of having completed an audit. Sadly, some subject leaders will do this and feel that they are being effective, when in actual fact they may be simply recording the fact that they are unaware of the full range of resources needed for their subject or are failing to meet the resourcing needs of the teachers and learners in their school. In actual fact, drawing up a list of the current resources is merely the first stage of the audit process.

There are a variety of ways in which you could access this information and the choice of method will depend on the size, context and organisation of your school. A few possible approaches are detailed below.

Central stock analysis

As previously mentioned, if there is a central store of curriculum resources then it may be a simple process of working through this stock and recording what is present. If you are going to use this technique then it is always wise to let colleagues know that you are planning to do so well in advance so that they can return any materials that have wrongly taken up residence in their classroom, car or garden shed. It is amazing how far resources can migrate across the course of a school year!

 **timesaver**

> If you are planning to conduct a central stock analysis, the collation of the initial list could be completed by a member of the support staff, as it is only the *analysis* of the completed list which requires the expertise of the subject leader.

Distributed audits

If the resources in your school are spread out over a large site, stored in different departments or are kept in classrooms (due to a lack of additional storage), then a distributed audit may be the most manageable method. Fundamentally, you will be asking colleagues to list the subject-specific resources that they have access to, enabling you to compile a whole school inventory of equipment and materials. As we are all busy people, colleagues may not appreciate being given a blank piece of paper to fill in, nor may they have the time to draw up their own exhaustive list of resources used to support teaching and learning in your subject. Therefore, produce a guide list of the types of resources you might expect to find for your

> little gems can be found during these kinds of audits

subject that can then be used as a quick and simple tick list for your colleagues, as they look around their classroom or hunt through cupboards. Providing this initial level of guidance may also encourage and help staff to identify other, less standard resources that have sat in the back of a cupboard for a long time because they had been forgotten or staff had failed to make the link between the resource and your subject. It is amazing what little gems can be found during these kinds of audits.

Hidden treasures audit

This kind of audit is excellent if, again, you do not have a central store of resources and have a moderately sized school with a number of parallel classes. To put it simply, as the subject leader, you would ask colleagues to make all the subject-specific resources they keep in their classrooms or regularly use available for you and other staff to view at a given time. You may choose to ask colleagues to bring them along to a staff meeting, or you may want to lead a 'treasure hunt' around the school during which you will visit different areas of the school where resources have been collated for viewing. Not only does this allow you as the subject leader to gain a clearer understanding of what resources are available, you are also able to assess the distribution of the resources across the school, identifying any departments and year groups that are over- or under-resourced. Such an opportunity can act as a reminder to all colleagues of the range of resources available to them for your subject. From experience, it is often these types of audit which will uncover the 'lost treasure' of resources or reveal that piece of equipment your colleagues have been hunting high and low to find.

Once you have established current resourcing levels, as well as the location and distribution of equipment, you can then take action. Remember to ask yourself: 'So what are the school's resourcing needs?' You may have sufficient experience to be able to identify the gaps in the resource provision and you can then use this information to make an approach to the school leadership team (SLT) for funding to support this.

brilliant tip

If you are asked by the SLT to submit a bid or proposal for curriculum funding, provide them with the Three Whats:

1 **What** the resource is.

2 **What** it will do to enhance teaching and learning.

3 **What** the cost will be (including postage and packing or any annual subscription fees).

Having this information at your fingertips will show that you have carefully considered this potential purchase and can effectively justify the expenditure.

If you still feel unsure about how best to proceed in order to secure effective resourcing for teaching and learning in your subject, you may need to look beyond your school. You could approach your local authority (LA) advisor in such instances, who should be able to offer a suggested list of resources that you can compare with the school's current audit of provision. Equally, it can often be helpful to compare notes with a leader of the same subject in another school or even equivalent leaders across your school cluster.

There is also another group of people who can always offer advice – your colleagues! Following your audit and having raised your colleagues' awareness about the resources available in the school, it is sometimes useful to ask staff to compile a wish-list of resources that would be helpful to them in teaching your specific subject. This can be an effective way of drawing upon your colleagues' expertise in teaching a specific year group (which may be unfamiliar to you) and combining this with your professional leadership of the specific subject area.

you should be able to prove that the resource offers value for money

One word of warning: make sure that staff can justify their requests, as there are many resources on the market which are very attractive and appealing to the eye but may actually have limited use within the curriculum. Your headteacher or school leadership team may well need a detailed justification to support the purchase of any resources you request. As the subject leader, you should be able to prove that the resource offers value for money and will have a positive impact on the quality of teaching and learning.

Auditing colleagues' skills, knowledge and understanding

It is worth remembering that a sufficient volume of high quality teaching resources alone will not automatically result in high quality teaching and learning. Even the best resourced school will struggle to maintain high standards in teaching and learning, if the staff using the resources lack sufficient skills, knowledge and understanding in the different aspects of the curriculum.

As educational professionals, we can assume that colleagues have achieved appropriate levels of expertise within the boundaries of the national curriculum, having successfully met NQT induction standards and skills assessments, as well as other forms of performance management, with associated continuing professional development (CPD). However, there will always be the need for further CPD as staff progress through their careers and encounter aspects of the curriculum in which they have less experience or confidence. For some, this might be the use of ICT in your subject, whereas others might require support in teaching your subject to a year group that they haven't yet taught.

brilliant tip

When devising an audit of your colleagues' skills, knowledge and understanding, remember to consider learning support staff. It is their job to support learning in the classroom and they too may benefit from structured training, which will further enhance the provision for the learners.

For each teacher, the required support will be slightly different as it is based on previous experiences in the subject, personal skills/ attributes and the aspects of curriculum they currently teach. The daunting prospect for some subject leaders is that they are expected to provide this support when they themselves might not be fully confident in all aspects of the subject or where there are personal concerns about advising and supporting a more experienced (in terms of time spent in the classroom) member of staff.

As with resources, when auditing staff skills, knowledge and understanding you must initially gather your information. What are the staff needs in my subject? The most effective way to gather this information is to talk to the staff themselves. However, the *way* in which this is done can have an impact on the usefulness of the information you gather. Here are some methods of gathering your information:

- Individual staff questionnaire with follow-up support.
- Whole staff meetings with skills, knowledge and understanding needs as an agenda item, prior to a series of further training sessions.
- Department, year group or small team meetings to discuss specific training needs, prior to a series of more closely tailored training sessions.

When considering which of these approaches to use, it is worthwhile mentioning that it may be appropriate to use more than one or even all these techniques to gain the full engagement of all the staff involved. It is important to remember that, dependent on your school context and the characteristics of the individual staff involved, discussion of professional training needs can be an emotive issue for some, as they may interpret this as exposing their professional weaknesses to their close colleagues. Sensitivity to staff sensibilities is therefore paramount and you, as the subject leader, should always seek to lead such discussions with a supportive and positive tone to foster a positive and professional atmosphere, thus encouraging the full involvement of all the staff.

Below is a helpful list of dos and don'ts when starting discussions about training needs and CPD with your staff.

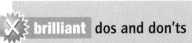 **dos and don'ts**

Do

✔ Draw up a list of basic skills, knowledge and understanding that you would expect all staff to have in your subject area, as a starting point for discussion.

✔ Share this list with the staff, ensuring that it is contextualised and fully explained.

✔ Remind colleagues that this is a form of continuing professional development and will help to ensure they are supported in providing the best for their learners.

✔ Encourage open discussion of training needs if appropriate, as staff may then learn that they aren't the only ones who struggle with particular aspects.

✔ Show sensitivity to the needs of individuals, making time to discuss specific needs privately if necessary.

Don't

✘ Make assumptions about the skills, knowledge and understanding of colleagues, positive or negative!

✘ Make individuals feel uncomfortable by discussing their specific needs with others, without their prior permission.

✘ Be afraid of being honest about your *own* needs in the subject, as this may help to develop an atmosphere of shared learning and collaborative development.

✘ Limit the audit to teaching staff – support staff may also benefit from curriculum training and will then be able to more effectively support teaching and learning.

✘ Expect everyone to be positive about the training – usually all staff will be committed but you may come up against resistance for both personal and professional reasons. In these cases, remember to reiterate the need for the training to ensure the best outcome for our learners. It is hard to argue with a rationale that is built on the core foundation of our profession!

When you have gathered the relevant information about the subject-specific training needs of your colleagues, it is important that you analyse the data from a whole school point of view, as well as on an individual basis. Working in this way you may find that trends emerge across the school, where groups of staff require the same or similar training, thus allowing you to target training for these individuals more effectively. This can be achieved by formally structuring small training groups which meet together with you for focused training, or by simply encouraging colleagues to informally meet to discuss their progress with training, as supportive friends. The subject leader must then decide who is best placed to lead the training for these individuals – it is not necessarily the case that the subject leader themselves should conduct training sessions.

However, in areas where you, as the subject leader, are confident in delivering specific training, then you should do so. This helps to build relationships with your colleagues in a leadership role which may be distinct from your other personal and professional relationships. It also helps you to maintain a 'feel' for the continuing training needs of the staff: for example, staff being trained may request further training as an off-shoot of the session you have led. Another source of in-house training may be other colleagues in the school.

use their expertise and share it

As a result of the skills audit, it may emerge that there is an individual member of staff, or even a group, with confidence/competence in an aspect of the curriculum that other staff have identified as a priority for their own development. As long as they are happy to do so, use their expertise and share it with the rest of the staff, through a series of staff meetings, arranging observations of teaching or establishing a programme of team teaching sessions where the confident staff are paired with less confident colleagues to plan, teach and review a lesson or series of lessons.

In some cases it may be necessary to request external training support. This is usually possible through LA advisors or representatives; however, there are also professional consultants who will work with schools to develop specific aspects of their curriculum. One potential barrier to this is the financial commitment required from the school, which can run into hundreds of pounds for half or whole day sessions. In order to mitigate these costs, it can be worthwhile considering whether there are other schools in the local area with teachers who would also benefit from such training, allowing the costs to be shared across a group of schools. It is in these circumstances that developing links and networks with colleagues in similar roles, in different schools, can really pay dividends!

Following any training that has taken place, it is essential for the subject leader to monitor and evaluate the outcomes for the learners in the school, in order to answer the question 'So what impact has the training had?' This can happen in a number of ways, including lesson observations, work sampling and discussions with learners (all of which will be addressed in subsequent chapters). This is a key element of continuing professional development, as it is a cyclical process whereby the training received by colleagues should improve the quality of teaching and learning in the classroom, from which further monitoring and evaluation can then be used to identify the next steps for training and additional CPD.

 **example**

Auditing ICT skills and securing improvement

Richard was an ICT subject leader at a large school, where interactive whiteboards had been installed in all learning areas. The teaching staff had been using the whiteboards to support their teaching for approximately 18 months, having received some initial technical training soon after the ▶

whiteboards had been installed. During a cycle of lesson observations within the school, focusing on the use of the new interactive whiteboards across the curriculum, it became apparent that all staff were confident in the basic operation of the technology but only some were seen to fully exploit the potential of their whiteboards to effectively enhance teaching and learning. Richard chose to work alongside one of the most confident staff to draw up a simple 'yes/no' staff skills audit questionnaire, incorporating those whiteboard skills that a limited number of more confident colleagues had effectively exhibited in their lesson observations. The questionnaire was then distributed to staff and the results analysed by Richard.

From his analysis, Richard identified at least one key strength which had been highlighted by each member of staff, ensuring that virtually the whole range of interactive whiteboard skills had been covered. He then held a meeting with all the staff, in which the wide range of skill sets amongst the staff was acknowledged, praised and appreciated. The fact that each member of staff had been identified as having at least one specific strength in this area resulted in a highly positive atmosphere, which was conducive to Richard's suggestion of a mutual training session. The structure of this style of training required each individual to provide some training to their colleagues. To this end, it was agreed that each member of staff would be given two weeks to put together a simple demonstration/presentation of the skill/s that they had identified as being a personal strength, rooted in their own class teaching, which they would be prepared to share with colleagues at the next staff meeting.

Over the subsequent fortnight, Richard received some requests for minimal additional support for colleagues in preparing their demonstrations – in the majority of cases they were simply asking for reassurance that the example they had selected from their teaching sufficiently exemplified the skill they had been asked to demonstrate.

In the mutual training session, each member of staff gave their demonstration to their colleagues, with the end result that all staff felt appreciated, and everyone learned at least one new skill. There was a hugely supportive atmosphere within the training session, as everyone was sharing a similar level of nervous excitement at the prospect of sharing their own technical expertise.

Richard was then able to focus his next round of lesson observations on the application of the new skills acquired in the training session to each teacher's own classroom practice. At a whole school level, the success of the ICT session resulted in the mutual training model being rolled out to incorporate other aspects of the whole school curriculum, including pastoral support.

 **brilliant** recap

The four most important messages from this chapter for the Brilliant Subject Leader are:

1   Take time to find out about your subject, before trying to take action.

2   Prioritise your actions. You may have a long list of priorities but start with those that will have the most significant impact on teaching and learning.

3   Don't be an island! Collaborate with colleagues in your own school, other schools and within the LA.

4   Remember the role that *all* staff have a role in developing your subject, including the often forgotten learning support staff!

CHAPTER 3

Curriculum planning

As a subject leader, it is vital that you possess a clear understanding of how teaching and learning is structured across the school. This includes age-appropriate expectations as well as the hierarchy of subject skills and curriculum breadth which is required by the national curriculum. It is a fact that a school cannot successfully provide consistently effective learning experiences in a subject where it lacks a clear curriculum structure. You may indeed have pockets of excellent teaching and learning in individual classrooms where teachers are adapting the curriculum to match the needs of their pupils; however, if this is not consistent across the school, you as the subject leader would fail in your duty of care for all learners in the school. It is therefore essential that curriculum planning is carefully structured, effectively delivered and rigorously monitored.

As a new or aspirant subject leader, you need to consider curriculum planning as the foundation on which good quality teaching and learning can be built. Essentially, build your teaching and learning on sand and it quickly loses coherence; whereas give it a foundation of granite and you can expect teaching to develop and learning to thrive across the school.

If you are new to the role then evaluating the quality and structure of the curriculum can be a good place to start, as this will not only help you to gain a whole school understanding of where your subject stands, it will also bring you into contact with your colleagues across the school. Hence, you will begin building and developing relationships with your colleagues in your new leadership role.

The foundations of curriculum planning

It may be helpful to provide some background to the school curriculum as a whole, as by understanding the nature of the beast you are then best placed to tame it. The way in which schools organise and structure their curriculum has undergone a number of significant changes in the last 20 years. Prior to the introduction of the national curriculum, schools organised learning in the way they thought was most suitable. There may have been guidance from the local authority, there may have been an agreed 'town' syllabus, but often the experiences in the classroom were dictated by the interests of the teacher. This sometimes resulted in excellent teaching in particular aspects of the curriculum – usually those that interested the teacher – but less consistency in other areas of learning. Many adults in their 30s and beyond may remember always covering the same topic in many different guises (I personally experienced most of my primary school curriculum through the medium of trees), or they may remember the teacher that always had time for a song but found geography skills harder to fit into the day! There was some excellence in teaching, and a lot of enjoyment on the part of the children, but often the curriculum lacked consistency and balance in coverage.

The impact of the national curriculum

The advent of the national curriculum in 1988 was intended to provide guidance on content and balance which helped many schools to generate their own schemes of work. These matched the expectations of the national curriculum and provided a more rounded experience for their learners, as there were now more meaningful links between subject areas.

However, in the 1990s it was still felt that some aspects of the curriculum lacked structure and uniformity across schools and thus the National Strategies were introduced for literacy and numeracy. Whilst these provided unprecedented detail about the content and structure of learning at a termly and weekly level, many schools found this overwhelming and began to compartmentalise learning in order to meet all the expectations now laid before them. This resulted in many of the previously meaningful links between core and foundation subjects being lost. For a brief period, it appeared that the educational world had developed an obsession for standardised national approaches which provided 'off-the-peg' learning experiences with the introduction of the QCA schemes of work. Whilst never being intended as a statutory curriculum, many schools latched onto the colourful folders, with bland grey curriculum content, in a daze created by the need to meet external guidance and rigid structures.

The situation today

Thankfully, we have now remembered that we could teach before folders of guidance and that we can be trusted to devise meaningful learning experiences of our own. Hence, we now find schools are freeing themselves of the shackles of planning dictated from a mysterious external body. They are beginning to create their own curriculum structures which, whilst meeting the statutory requirements of the national curriculum, can reflect the context of their school, the needs of their learners and the interests of their teachers.

As a result, this is a very exciting time for subject leaders. We have been empowered to innovate with the curriculum, to look at stimulating new ways of engaging pupils and to find meaningful approaches to education for the twenty-first century and beyond. That said, as

> this is a very exciting time for subject leaders

the sole leader of a subject in school, achieving these goals can sometimes seem intimidating, as your decisions will impact on every pupil in the school and many, if not all, of your colleagues.

Evaluating the whole school, subject specific curriculum

It would be foolish to suggest to you that in your new role you should erase any trace of the existing curriculum and start from scratch. It is probably the case that the present curriculum at your school is the result of the progressive input of a large number of professionals who were all trying to achieve the best for the school. It is therefore sensible to evaluate the curriculum through the eyes of a teacher in the current educational climate, further embedding the relevant, valuable and effective aspects and then investing time to redevelop those areas which are weaker or no longer pertinent.

brilliant tip

When evaluating the curriculum, don't do so in isolation. Obviously you should utilise the experience, expertise and understanding of colleagues within the school, but also consider the pupils in the school. They will have an opinion too – and it is their curriculum after all!

Evaluate criteria

Nationally and even globally there are numerous emerging opinions about what makes a good quality curriculum. If you tried to incorporate all current thinking then you would probably end up with a very disjointed and conflicting one. Therefore, here are some of the common key quality indicators of a successful curriculum:

- Is there progression in learning?
- Is there a balance between the acquisition and development of new knowledge, understanding and skills?
- Is the curriculum relevant to our school context? Does it reflect our social, cultural and (where relevant) religious demographic?
- Is the curriculum suitably 'global'? Does it prepare our pupils for the diverse and rapidly changing world we live in?
- Does it result in high standards of academic achievement?
- Do pupils enjoy their learning?
- Does the school curriculum meet any national or local statutory requirements, such as the national curriculum or locally agreed syllabi?
- Are pupils encouraged and enabled to make a positive contribution to their school, local, national and international communities?
- Where appropriate, are safe and healthy lifestyles promoted?
- Does the curriculum foster economic wellbeing amongst pupils?

In viewing these criteria, it may be helpful to also have some understanding of their origins. All schools subject to OFSTED inspections are expected to be able to demonstrate the effective implementation of the five outcomes detailed in the 'Every Child Matters' framework published in 2004. These five outcomes are intended to ensure that all children are given the opportunity and support to develop skills in:

- keeping themselves safe;
- maintaining a healthy lifestyle;
- making a positive contribution to their communities at all scales;
- maintaining economic wellbeing;

- enjoying their education as a platform for a rewarding adulthood.

The other elements of the evaluative criteria stem from the long-standing, academically researched and practically applied principles of what constitutes good quality learning. This is important to remember, as with any period of innovation, there will undoubtedly be some experimentation with more faddish techniques and curriculum structures. However, as a subject leader, if you can hold on to the evaluative criteria above, and keep the child at the centre of everything you do, then you will be able to distinguish between valuable new practice and passing fads.

Armed with your evaluative criteria and sticking true to your child-centred approach to learning, you should now be able to ask yourself the first of two key questions in relation to the subject curriculum you are charged to lead: 'Is the structure, content and scope of our planning effective?' This is a question that you should only attempt to answer once you have gathered all the facts. It would be 'easier' to merely collect all planning documentation from across the school, read through it all and then independently decide what works and what doesn't. However, you must remember that you are reviewing and evaluating the subject curriculum you lead, not own. The ownership of the curriculum should always sit first with the pupils who will experience it, secondly with the teachers who adapt and deliver it, and third and finally with the leader who monitors and evaluates it.

the role of the subject leader in evaluating the curriculum is vital

Despite being third in the proposed hierarchy, the role of the subject leader in evaluating the curriculum is vital. It is you who will initially form an opinion of the effectiveness of the curriculum, but you will also seek the views of others within the school community before synthesising the differing views and opinions into one final evaluative statement.

Involving colleagues

There are numerous mechanisms that you could use to collate the information you need about the curriculum: however, you should always choose carefully to ensure the minimum impact on your time and that of others, in order to gain the maximum benefit for the school. One effective means of starting an evaluation of curriculum content and structure is to arrange a forum-style meeting. Notify your colleagues of your intention to review the curriculum well in advance, ensuring that there is the clear and verbalised purpose of securing the best experiences for the pupils in the classroom. This will allow them time to reflect on what currently works, what change is required and, importantly, how this change might happen. You could also ask them to seek the views of the pupils in the interim, which would also add to the subsequent discussion.

Following this period of self-reflection, the forum meeting can then be held, chaired by you as the subject leader. The formality of the meeting is important, as there is potential for this event to turn into a 'talking shop' where colleagues will invariably begin to focus solely on the negative aspects of the curriculum and their role, without taking suitable time to celebrate the current successes. The outcome of the meeting may also be diluted due to this lack of focus. Depending on the social and professional dynamics of your staff, you may wish to implement an 'issue and solution' approach to the meeting, whereby anyone raising a negative point about the curriculum should also be able to offer a solution or opportunity to instigate change. By working in this way you will be able to draw upon the expertise and contextual knowledge of your colleagues, whilst also engendering a positive team spirit where everyone feels involved in a process that will undoubtedly impact on their day-to-day work in the classroom.

You may feel pressurised to be able to offer answers to all the questions raised at the meeting, but this is unnecessary. By arranging such a gathering you are already acknowledging the importance of collaboration and taking time to reflect; as the subject leader you are facilitating the process of curriculum evaluation. Attempting to immediately troubleshoot the issues raised at the meeting might lead to hasty or impractical decisions, which may ultimately prove just as ineffective as the problems they were intended to solve. As well as proving to be a waste of time, this may impact on your colleagues' view of you as a strong and considerate subject leader.

Instead, listen carefully to the points raised and the associated discussion, but then take time to reflect on the state of the curriculum and research possible answers. Set a specific date and time at which you will reconvene the meeting to discuss the next steps for the curriculum.

Again, you should not feel the weight of providing the solutions alone. You may well have formed some innovative and exciting approaches to the curriculum and wish to implement these in response to the issues raised by your staff. However, you might find that your ideas can be enhanced and further developed with some extra time committed to additional research. This does not necessarily mean spending all your free time scouring the internet with infinite search terms

you are a leader within a community of leaders

(although there are many considerate local authorities who will publish work in their schools through their websites): remember that you are a leader within a community of leaders. Within your cluster of schools or, more broadly, the schools contained within your local authority, you will not be the only subject leader who is facing or has already faced curriculum issues similar to your own. If you are unsure which specific schools or individuals might be able to share their experiences or share the load by collaborating with you on a curriculum development project, then ask the local authority advisors. In their position, they are privileged to be able to regularly visit a range of different schools and should be able to point you in the direction of a supportive colleague.

The benefit of working in this way, especially if the colleague in question has already resolved the issues to the satisfaction of their school, is that you are again *working smarter, not harder*! You will be able to avoid the potential mistakes or blind alleys of enquiry that your colleague pursued, and instead use your time to more effectively address the issue in your school. There may also be the possibility of your colleague sharing research, working papers or even copies of the renewed subject cur- riculum structure and planning.

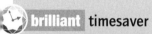 **brilliant** timesaver

When working with colleagues in other schools, it is helpful to receive any planning materials they choose to share in electronic format. Not only does this cut down on the number of trees used but it also means you can easily adapt the content for your own purposes or transfer it onto your own school planning formats.

A word of warning here: it can be very tempting to take the gift of another school's curriculum planning and attempt to implement it in your school in the same form. But remember that the best subject curriculum reflects the priorities, context and dynamics of that particular school, so always take time to carefully review any work shared by colleagues from other schools and adapt this to meet your specific requirements or ways of working.

Schemes of work

Similarly, there is an ever-growing range of published schemes of work for all curriculum subjects on the market. Each one possesses its own strengths and weaknesses but none should ever be used as an 'off-the-peg' solution to your curriculum structure and planning. If you are considering using a published curriculum scheme, then it is worthwhile requesting inspection copies from a range of different companies which you can share with colleagues. In this way, you can choose the scheme that has the greatest degree of versatility, in that it would allow teachers to easily adapt and amend the plans (many now come with accompanying CD-ROMs with adaptable electronic copies of the published documentation) and that can best serve the needs and context of the school.

Planning your curriculum

When you have gathered all the information relevant to your evaluation of the curriculum and the next steps for its development, you should then be able to answer the second key question: 'How could planning be further enhanced?' Whilst you will have devised a clear plan in your mind of how your subject curriculum should be further embedded and developed, you must remember that you are not the sole decision maker in this process. You must also seek input and, ultimately, approval from the senior school leadership team.

The requirements for subject leaders to liaise with senior leaders will differ from school to school, with the degree of subject leader autonomy varying greatly. However, as curriculum provision is an essential element of the school self-evaluation process, your deputy head and/or headteacher will need to be informed of your proposed changes. It is always better to be able to provide the senior school leadership with a full package of information, which includes a summary of how you evaluated the curriculum, the issues that were raised and, most importantly, a clear and achievable plan of how you intend to implement change. In doing so, you will present yourself as a strategic leader who has carefully devised an approach to meet the needs of the school at present; this fosters a degree of confidence in you as a leader and means they are more likely to agree to your plans. Their feedback will also provide you with the confidence that your goals and means of achieving them are supported by the school as a whole, which will help to convince any sceptical members of your team at the pre-planning team meeting.

▶ brilliant example

Developing a 'skills based' Science curriculum

Keshini was the Science subject leader of a large school. For a number of years, the school had been following the suggested, but not statutory, scheme of work for Science. The teaching staff had always been generally happy with the scheme of work as it provided a clear series of lesson plans for each aspect of the Science curriculum and aided them in structuring the broader curriculum across the academic year.

Upon its introduction, Keshini had ensured that staff was aware of the scheme's optional nature and that they should adapt the planning to suit the needs of their class. More recently, however, a large number of less experienced staff had joined the team and they had begun to follow the provided planning more rigidly, with less critical evaluation of whether adapting it could make the learning experiences more applicable to the pupils in their classes.

In conjunction with this change, Keshini was also becoming increasingly aware of the shift that was taking place in the focus of national qualifications and curriculum tests towards developing scientific skills as a priority. When she revisited the local authority approved scheme, she found that scientific skills development in her school did not have a sufficiently high focus in comparison with the development of knowledge and understanding. It became apparent that the way in which she and her colleagues structured the Science curriculum was in need of review. ▶

In order to achieve this, she first arranged a staff meeting where she asked her colleagues to look at the current scheme with 'fresh eyes', focusing in particular on identifying the existing opportunities to develop the full range of scientific skills. It soon became clear to them, as it had with Keshini, that the opportunities were severely limited. After some discussion of possible solutions, it was agreed that Keshini would contact local-cluster and out-of-cluster colleagues to establish how they were tackling this currently national issue.

Following a series of meetings with these colleagues, they decided to form a working party with Keshini in order to tackle the issue of scientific skills development within the curriculum. Over a period of weeks, with the support of their headteachers, the working party extracted the strongest element of the existing scheme, incorporated elements of other published schemes that the group had assembled for evaluation and devised a new structure for the curriculum.

It was then agreed, again with the support of the headteachers, that to help the teaching staff understand the importance of the scientific skills and how they should be incorporated, each Science subject leader in the working party would produce an example unit of work, into which they would weave skills, knowledge and understanding.

The final stage in the project involved the headteachers taking part in the working party arranging a shared staff development day. During this event, all staff who taught Science in each school gathered together and reviewed the example units of work produced by the group of subject leaders. Following this, the staff were allowed the time to work collaboratively with their own school staff or with colleagues from other schools to write the full scheme in its entirety, using the broader guidelines produced by the working party. This ultimately led to the development of a 'town' Science scheme of work and facilitated further cross-cluster work between different classes of pupils working in collaborative scientific research projects.

Monitoring and evaluating the impact of curriculum developments

In an ideal world, we as subject leaders would be able to communicate a clear plan, series of expectations and desired outcome to our colleagues and it would simply happen with no further input. Unfortunately, when you combine the daily pressures of working in a vibrant and often unpredictable school environment with the need to change planning practices to achieve the outcomes of curriculum evaluation and review, the new processes which initially require more time and thought on behalf of the teaching staff are often the first to fall by the wayside.

Therefore, regular and rigorous monitoring and evaluation of planning by the subject leader is of paramount importance. When approaching this as a leadership task, it is important to remember three guidelines. Any and all monitoring of planning should:

1 be achievable by the subject leader within reasonable time constraints;

2 not generate further unnecessary paperwork for teaching staff;

3 have an outcome which has a positive impact on the quality of curriculum planning.

To make the task of monitoring curriculum planning manageable for you in your role as subject leader, it can also be helpful to choose a relevant focus for the monitoring rather than trying to evaluate every possible aspect of the teachers' planning. For example, you may choose to focus on the explicit references to detailing of differentiation of learning within the plan or the degree to which the lesson content within the body of the plan meets the agreed school scheme of work. Choosing a focus means that you

> choose a relevant focus for the monitoring

can look in detail at specific elements of an individual teacher's planning, as well as conducting comparative evaluations between different teams, year groups or individual teachers.

When choosing a timescale for your monitoring, you will need to consider the type of planning you intend to examine. For example, if you are evaluating medium-term planning then a sampling period of every six to eight weeks might be appropriate; whereas when monitoring weekly/daily planning you might wish to take a sample of all planning for a period of weeks to give a more detailed snapshot of standards of documentation across the school. Whatever your chosen timescale, it is important that you communicate your intention to conduct this monitoring well in advance to ensure that planning is available from staff when you need it. All too often, subject leaders fail to do this, with the result that the sample is due the very day that a staff member has left their planning folder at home or the temperamental department printer breaks down.

Just as with any other form of monitoring and evaluation, the prospect of their planning and associated documentation being reviewed by a subject leader or senior member of staff can be a worrying one for teachers. This concern can grow if no feedback is given to the teaching staff, engendering feelings of self-doubt and suspicions about the motivation of the subject leader. Most schools have standardised means by which this type of feedback should be given, to ensure consistency in the work of their subject leaders across the school. However, regardless of the specific process, document or methodology, there are some guiding principles which should always be followed. When providing feedback on curriculum planning you should aim to:

- provide verbal feedback within 48 hours;
- provide some form of written feedback to each member of staff, as they may wish to use this as a record for their standards for performance management or promotion purposes;

- highlight positive aspects of the planning documentation, explaining why these elements are of value, to ensure staff morale is maintained;

- highlight all areas of development in direct relation to the focus of the planning, selecting one or two aspects which require more urgent attention: this means that if you raise one of the minor areas of development in the future, the member of staff is aware that it has already been acknowledged previously;

- provide the member of staff the opportunity to give either a verbal or written response to your feedback, thus enabling them to seek further support from you as their subject leader if necessary.

 **brilliant** recap

The four most important messages from this chapter for the Brilliant Subject Leader are:

1 Utilise the community of leaders around you: they are either experiencing the same challenges as you or may have even overcome them.

2 Take time to reflect on information and formulate a careful strategic plan before taking action: errors in judgement can take a long time to rectify once implemented at a whole school level.

3 Your school has a vibrant soul and personality of its own: this should be reflected in the curriculum content, so avoid off-the-peg solutions unless they can be appropriately adapted to meet your needs.

4 Approach your senior leadership team with the initial problems and your coherent solutions: thus they are more likely to agree with and support your ideas.

CHAPTER 4

Lesson observation

esson observation. These two words can often strike fear into teachers. Many assume that the considerable trepidation that can result from formalised observation is felt only by the individual being observed. In actual fact, having worked with numerous professionals in the same situation, and based on my own experience, the observer can also suffer from worries over the process of observation.

Whilst the subject of the observation can feel under pressure to 'put on a show', giving an all-singing, all-dancing demonstration of their ability to perform as an effective classroom teacher, you as the subject leader observing the classroom practice can also feel under a degree of pressure to perform in your leadership role. Understanding these pressures and acknowledging that we have all shared these worries at one time in the past can help all new and aspiring subject leaders to become more confident in evaluating classroom practice.

This chapter will lead you, as a new subject leader, through the process of lesson observation but I feel it is important to first explicitly address the common concerns expressed by subject leaders. As a result, you will hopefully be able to focus more sharply on lesson observation as a tool for personal professional development as well as an important aspect of school self-evaluation.

The worries shared by new subject leaders are explored below.

How do I know what makes a quality lesson?

The answer to this question will differ slightly from school to school. However, regardless of context, each school should have their own agreed evaluation schedule for teaching and learning. In much the same way as OFSTED have established agreed criteria for making judgements about teaching and learning, your school should have a similar set of criteria. These may be expressed in the school's teaching and learning policy; they may be detailed in a staff handbook; they could take the form of an agreed methodology for all learning spaces; or they are often used to form the body of the school's standard lesson observation record-keeping format. Their format is less relevant than the confidence they can offer a subject leader, as you can then feel assured that you are operating with the same expectations as every other leader in the school.

How can I make a judgement about another professional, when I am still refining my own practice?

Whilst there are many experienced teachers who are truly excellent classroom teachers, experience alone does not automatically result in good classroom practice. Any good teacher will acknowledge that they are never truly masters of the art; we are always learning, we are always reflecting on our practice and we are always aiming to improve our provision for the learners in our classroom. As mentioned in previous chapters, you are not intended to be the world's expert in your chosen subject but you are the individual who will place all aspects of the subject under a lens to evaluate standards, achievement and provision. In this role you are a valuable second pair of eyes, who can support colleagues to look more objectively at their own practice. The process should be collaborative and encourage partnership between colleagues, rather than one being forced to sit in judgement on another.

you are a valuable second pair of eyes

How will I deal with the situation if the lesson doesn't go well?

We must accept that, whilst the unpredictable nature of learning and pupils' varying responses to classroom teaching can be some of the most stimulating aspects of the profession, they will also sometimes result in lessons which don't go to plan. I can recall a number of lessons which I would rather forget and occasions when I have been grateful that no other professionals were observing my practice. From time to time, an observed lesson won't progress as planned and learning can be affected as a result. Again, in your role as a subject leader, you should work in collaboration with colleagues to hold a light to the issues but also provide support in securing improvement. In these situations more than any other, it is the quality of the dialogue between professionals that can make all the difference. This will be explored in more depth later in the chapter (see page 65).

I am going to be observing a close friend – will this cause problems?

There is one simple mantra to keep in mind in these situations – *keep personal and professional lives separate*. Whilst you might enjoy a Friday night drink with a colleague, as soon as you step into their classroom in your role as subject leader you must maintain a professional outlook. Making this distinction throughout the observation process can help to ease any issues around conducting the observation and providing feedback. It also means that any discussions of the observation process end at the school door; don't bring it up over your Saturday night curry and, equally, don't allow yourself to be drawn into similar conversations when you're at the weekend barbeque. Both you and your friend/colleague are professionals who have entered into teaching to secure the best education for the children in their care and it is this that professional judgements and discussions should always remain focused on.

If correctly approached, the process of lesson observation can provide all parties with excellent professional development and can have a significant impact on the experiences of learners in the classroom. It is a direct form of support and, in some cases, intervention which can have a virtually immediate impact on the provision in individual classrooms. It can be a professionally challenging and, at times, a difficult task, but one that is certainly worthwhile and valuable for the pupils in our schools.

Preparing to observe teaching and learning

As with any complex task, the success of classroom observation can often rely on the quality of the preparation prior to the task. Observing teaching and learning is not simply a case of arriving at the classroom door, staying for the duration of the lesson and then leaving with a polite 'thank you'.

Just like the other forms of monitoring and evaluation we have discussed so far, lesson observation must have a clearly defined purpose. The purpose can vary from observation to observation, but all professionals involved in the process should understand the intended outcome of the process. In most cases, you will be initiating a lesson observation as a means of monitoring the standards of teaching and learning in your subject. For example, it might be a response to a new initiative you have implemented, establishing how it is being transferred into the classroom.

everyone involved in the process should benefit

Alternatively, you may be auditing an aspect of curriculum provision, wishing to gain an insight into classroom practice through your observation. In some situations, a teacher may have requested the lesson observation as a form of professional development or to seek advice about a challenging situation/individual. As long as the purpose is clear, then everyone involved in the process should benefit.

It is essential that the teacher being observed is given the opportunity to have some input into preparation for the observation and also to explicitly agree to the basic principles/goals of the observation. Not only does this ensure that the teacher feels involved in this professionally relevant and important process, but it also means that should any serious issues arise, the teacher cannot explain them away as being the result of a lack of clarity in the observation process (for example, a teacher excusing the ineffective use of support staff in the lesson because he/she was not aware that this was a focus for the observation).

Whilst most schools will have an agreed observation protocol, detailing the before, during and after expectations of the subject leader and the professional being observed, it is useful to clarify some of the steps you might take prior to entering the classroom for the observation. These could include:

Give sufficient notice

The longer the better, as teachers can then structure their weekly timetable appropriately should small changes be needed to accommodate the observation.

If giving a term's notice of an observation, then also remember to confirm arrangements closer to the actual date to ensure that it hasn't been overlooked in the often hectic weekly planning processes.

Agree how long the lesson will last

This will allow you to evaluate the teacher's use of time and pace in their lesson, as well as ensure that you don't miss an aspect of or the entire observation. Your colleague may well have invested extra time and effort in preparing this lesson, so make sure you are there on time and stay until the end! It can also be worthwhile notifying administrative staff that you will be observing for a given period and cannot be disturbed, so that

> make sure you are there on time and stay until the end

they don't assume that because you are not teaching a class you can come to the phone or speak to a visitor who has just arrived at the school.

Agree the focus/topic

Clarify what you will be looking for and why, establish if there is anything specific that your colleague would like feedback on and share the criteria that will be used to make any judgements. By doing this explicitly, it can help you to clarify your thinking prior to the observation, and will also help to calm or reassure a potentially nervous colleague as they will know very clearly what they are aiming to achieve.

Provide your colleague with a copy of the record-keeping form

Again, this will help to ease your colleagues' nerves as they will have a better understanding of what you might be scribbling down at the back of the classroom. From experience, the process of copying the blank document for a colleague also gives you the opportunity to ensure that you have a copy ready for the actual observation. It is all too easy for other professional duties to take priority on the day of the observation, meaning that you suddenly need to go straight into the classroom to observe but are without the paperwork you need. This results in you either being late for the observation or feeling very unprepared and unsettled as you enter the room.

Share the observation etiquette with your colleague

Agree where you will sit during any direct teaching activities, establish your level of involvement with the learning that will take place, etc. These will be explored in more detail later in this chapter (see page 56). It can also be reassuring to share with your colleague that you may/may not be engaging with them through smiles or nods, etc., during the lesson. This will depend on your style of observation – whether you prefer to remain detached during the observation or feel comfortable in giving reassuring smiles. Regardless of your personal style, explicitly share this with your colleague so that they do not misconstrue your steely gaze as a sign that things aren't going well.

Collect a copy of the planning for the lesson

This will help to avoid any disruption of pace and learners' focus at the start of the actual observation while, for example, the teacher tries to deliver paperwork to you across the room. It is also important to establish with your colleague the weighting you will assign to the planning, as a component of the observation. For example, is the planning merely to help you, as the subject leader, understand the over-arching structure of the lesson or will you be looking closely at the relationship between the planned teaching sequence and the reality of the delivery in the classroom?

brilliant tip

The pressures of a busy workload can mean it is easy to delay reviewing lesson planning and other documentation that a teacher may have provided in connection with your observation until you actually enter the classroom to start the observation. However, if you are then desperately trying to comprehend the complex planning as the lesson begins, you may well miss some important elements of the lesson. Take time to read the planning through carefully prior to the lesson. You will then feel more prepared to observe as you will already have some idea of the structure and content of the lesson, allowing you to focus on the way in which the lesson meets the agreed observation criteria.

Additional benefits

From your perspective as a subject leader, the process of lesson observation can also help to maintain the *work smarter, not harder* approach to your role, by providing you with additional insights into your subject area. For example, whilst you might be observing a lesson with an ostensible focus on the teacher's use of assessment for learning principles, you might simultaneously begin to gain an insight into resourcing needs for your subject, or how effectively the planning process supports the practical aspects of teaching and learning. You must maintain your agreed focus as your prime purpose of the observation, but there is nothing to stop you making your own additional observations which, although not relevant to the feedback for the teacher, might suggest future lines of enquiry or highlight emerging subject priorities.

Observing teaching and learning

As a new subject leader entering a classroom to observe for the first time, it can be a slightly uncomfortable experience. This can be partially due to the fact that a classroom is essentially an individual teacher's territory and, in a primitive sense, you are an outsider moving into that territory. In some instances, there may be an additional degree of discomfort if the teacher's understandable nerves manifest themselves either as coldness towards you or over-sensitivity to your needs. Meeting prior to the observation can help to ease some of these issues but, nevertheless, the situation can often feel daunting to subject leaders.

To help combat these feelings it can be helpful to put yourself into the observation mindset as soon as you enter the room. Greet the teacher, other adults and pupils (if appropriate within the agreed observation etiquette/protocols) and then, rather than standing awkwardly in a corner, move directly to your agreed seating position.

An obvious choice when choosing the observer's seat is to place yourself at the back of the classroom. Professionals often feel that this keeps them out of the eye-line of the pupils, hence avoiding unnecessary distraction and providing an overview of the classroom. However, this distant rear position can also limit your effectiveness as an observer. Remember that you are observing *teaching and learning*. Therefore you need to be able to observe *the teacher and the learners*. All too often, subject leaders will observe the actions and responses of the teacher from a rear position, but then are unable to fully judge the response of the learners, as only the backs of their heads are visible.

Instead, consider moving to a side-on position. This will allow you to genuinely see the interaction between teacher and learner: you will be able to observe any pupils who may be

> see the interaction between teacher and learner

passively disengaged with learning, and also whether the teacher acknowledges this and addresses it. Equally, you will be able to judge how the teacher effectively uses the responses from the pupils to dynamically modify and structure their direct teaching activities.

As previously discussed, every school should have some form of agreed observation criteria that can be used to standardise the expectations of subject leaders and senior leaders, across the school, when conducting observations of teaching and learning. However, as a professional new to subject leadership it may be helpful to review some of the headline aspects of quality teaching and learning when making judgements of colleagues' classroom practice.

During the lesson, a subject leader should be considering the following components, looking at them in isolation as well as in the context of the lesson as a whole.

Has the teacher introduced the focus for today's learning?

This might be in the form of a shared learning objective; it might be shared through a stimulus activity such as peer discussion; or it could be displayed for the pupils to read themselves.

Has the teacher made reference to how this lesson links to prior learning?

The teacher may do so explicitly themselves or use questioning to elicit responses from the pupils and to help them to recall previous learning.

Do pupils understand the relevance and purpose of their learning?

This can often be judged through the pupils' responses to the teacher's questioning. However, it is also important for the observer to seek out those children who may have been less communicative during whole class teaching, establishing whether they too have understood the purpose of the lesson. If they haven't, then consider whether the teacher is aware of this. As a professional, it is all too tempting to 'fill in' any gaps in learning that you become aware of, on a one-to-one basis, during an observation. However, by doing so you are robbing the teacher of the chance to demonstrate their classroom management and awareness of the needs of their pupils. Instead, you could direct the child to seek the support of the teacher or another adult and then observe the result.

Does the planning and subsequent teaching show evidence of assessment for learning?

This could be observed through the use of effective questioning to draw out pupils' understanding or responding to a specific pupil's misconceptions and utilising this as a teaching point to clarify, consolidate and further the learning for all. It could also be possible to evidence this through modifications to planning. Some teachers are opposed to scribbling over their carefully word-processed planning; however, it is the process of annotating planning and adapting subsequent lessons in response to reflecting on previous learning that can result in effective practice. By doing so, the teacher is being effective in meeting the needs of all pupils and is personalising the learning to the specific requirements of his/her class.

Are links made across the curriculum, with opportunities to apply skills in meaningful contexts?

In the current climate of curriculum innovation and the unarguable principle of ensuring that learning is meaningful to all learners in our schools, it is essential that teachers aim to link learning. This can be as simple as encouraging pupils to make use of their high level literacy skills when recording and concluding a scientific investigation, or applying mathematical understanding to calculate the differences between their personal best and that of a peer in an athletics session.

Exploiting links between subjects can make the broader experience of school more meaningful for our pupils. It is also a challenge for teachers in secondary schools in particular, which subject leaders can offer support in overcoming, as they need to look beyond their department or specialist subject and work to raise their awareness of the broader curriculum being experienced by the learners they encounter in one or two lessons over a week.

Remember, however, caution is needed in making these links to ensure that they are supportive of the main learning objective for the session and do not cloud the focus of the lesson for the learner.

Do the learners have some influence or choice about what is being learnt?

When observing a lesson, it is sometimes difficult to immediately see if opportunities for learners to express their pupil voice have been incorporated, because the main structure, pace and direction of the lesson is rightly set and guided by the teacher. However, there are aspects where you might be able to easily see this element of choice through activities in which the pupils are empowered to choose which aspect of a broader teacher-selected topic they wish to research, through how they choose to present their research findings, or how they choose to organise their specific responsibilities within a group/collaborative working environment.

Overall, the teacher should be the principle guide and director of learning, but will also work in collaboration with their pupils rather than dictating every minute aspect of the learning process.

Does the teacher have a good knowledge of the subject and progression within it?

This is not asking you as an observer to gather evidence that the teacher is aware of every aspect of their given curriculum, at every given moment. For the purposes of the lesson observation, you should simply focus on whether the lesson and the learning it contains fits appropriately into a broader sequence of lessons and whether, within this specific lesson, the teacher demonstrates confident and accurate subject knowledge. It is also possible to gain some insight into the teacher's understanding of subject knowledge and skills progression, if they are able to effectively meet the needs of all learners through, for example, accelerating the learning of the more able and simplifying or consolidating learning for the less able.

Does the teacher give pupils time to explore their thoughts?

This is an aspect of the observation that must be dealt with sensitively. In some cases, if a teacher is newly qualified, less experienced or finds observation very stressful then they can tend to resort to attempting to control every aspect of the lesson, including the pupils' responses. In extreme cases, teachers might feel pressurised by time and find themselves falling into a pattern of asking questions which they then proceed to answer themselves, for fear of the pupils not providing the desired response. Equally, some teachers can rely too heavily on specific, often more able pupils, who can be 'relied' upon to get the answer right.

Therefore, as a subject leader, you may need to make a professional judgement on whether any issues which arise in this area are a genuine concern or are due to nerves. This will affect how you address this aspect in the feedback after the lesson.

Opportunities that teachers can provide to allow pupils to explore their thoughts can include brief periods of peer discussion around a given topic or question (no more than a few minutes), with feedback expected afterwards. The teacher might also allow time for individuals to reflect on their own understanding and to devise questions which might help to clarify aspects of their learning, or hold longer group discussion sessions in a more formalised structure where pupils are assigned roles to help organise the conversation.

Are there positive relationships between adults and children which are conducive to learning?

During your observation, you will be able to get a sense of the general atmosphere in the classroom and what the atmosphere for learning in this particular class might be like beyond this isolated observation. Relationships and the degree to which they are warm and supportive can be hard to quantify but easy to see when present.

get a sense of the general atmosphere

For example, a teacher's tone with their pupils can reveal much of their general approach to the group as a whole. If a teacher is heavily sarcastic, then this may suggest an atmosphere where pupils fear ridicule and may not engage with learning opportunities as fully as possible. On the other hand, the pupils may understand and respond to the teacher's humour so that it actually supports learning and positive relationships. Another example might be a teacher who openly acknowledges when they have made a mistake, such as a spelling or calculation error, and this in turn creates an atmosphere where the pupils too feel comfortable in 'having a go' at a new learning experience, without fear of failure. There are no definitive models of positive learning relationships; it is a case of experiencing the life of the classroom during the observation and making a judgement based on your findings.

Is the classroom environment well organised, stimulating and presented in a way which scaffolds the learning process and celebrates success?

This is one of the easiest aspects to judge during an observation as it is all around you. Ideally, you would be looking to find a classroom that comprises more than just a whiteboard, desks and chairs; you would hope that the subject you lead is presented in an interactive and vibrant manner in the classroom. Are there learning prompts displayed around the room? Are there tools and materials available which support pupils in taking responsibility for their own learning? Is it possible to see that the learning process is valued – i.e. skills development, preparation for projects? This is of particular importance, as it is not only the work which presents the best handwriting which should be celebrated, but also the outcomes of children who may have had to be more resilient or resourceful in their learning than others, to achieve their final goal.

What overall comments can you make about learning, progress and standards?

When considering the lesson as a whole, it is important to reflect on the causal link between teaching, learning and progress/achievement/standards. If, in your observations, you are beginning to find evidence for effective teaching, then it should follow that the learning, in the majority of cases, is also effective. There may be specific children who may need to be highlighted to the teacher, such the 'invisible' child who can easily slip through the net because they are very reserved, or the individual who always appears to understand but doesn't, or those that are expert at avoiding learning – but overall, teaching and learning are positive.

Alternatively, if there are emerging signs that a large number of pupils aren't engaged with the lesson or aren't achieving what they are capable of due to lack of challenge or poor assessment for learning, then it would be difficult to argue a case for the quality of the teaching to be good. You must remember that by first gathering the evidence about the smaller building blocks of effective teaching and learning, you will then be able to form a more rounded judgement of the big picture for that teacher and for you as a subject leader.

It is also good practice to try to avoid making a summary judgement immediately after the lesson. During the observation it is a good idea to make a note of any questions you have as you observe, such as 'Why was Timothy sitting on his own for the duration of the lesson?' or 'Why didn't the teacher present the learning objective at the start of the session?' By asking the questions and carrying them forward for discussion with your colleague in the feedback meeting, then you will be able to gather *all* the relevant evidence before making an overall judgement. This is important as, by

> gather *all* the relevant evidence before making an overall judgement

not asking the right questions and presuming you understand all aspects of the lesson and how the teacher managed the learning, you may actually make an incorrect judgement. For example, it could be reasonable for Timothy to be sitting on his own due to a specific special need which makes it difficult for him to focus in a group situation and so the teacher has taken action to support his learning style. Alternatively, he might be a victim of social segregation or bullying and the teacher has failed to acknowledge this and, thus, has not provided the correct form of support. The facts of this situation could be established in open discussion with the teacher, after the observation, but without this, presumptions could cause issues for:

- you, because the teacher may be led to doubt the validity of your judgement;

- the teacher as they may not receive the support they need to develop their practice;

- the child, who may or may not be receiving appropriate in-class academic and/or pastoral care.

It is a good idea to have formed a view of the quality of teaching and learning in advance, based on what you have seen, but the feedback meeting should be used to help formalise this judgement and to ensure accuracy in your findings.

brilliant timesaver

There is much to remember during an observation and it is easy to miss something which you need to know to inform your judgement. Rather than having to waste time after the observation collecting further evidence, follow the checklist below to help you to make the most of the valuable time spent observing in the classroom.

- Remember to look at the children's work. Note down the names of any children whose work you might wish to sample later, to provide evidence for marking, progression, etc.

- Make a note of any specific utterances from the children which will support your findings.

- If necessary, take a step back from the lesson to review your notes – don't become another teaching assistant!

- Move around the classroom to experience what is happening around the teacher, as well as what the group or individual is doing in the corner. Has a group gone to work elsewhere? Follow them, as they are still part of the learning.

- Are there any children with special educational needs (SEN), English as an additional language (EAL) or on the gifted and talent register (GAT)? Are their needs being addressed?

- Talk to the children. Do they see the purpose of the learning? Are they enjoying the lesson?

- Keep thinking – Teaching, Learning, Achievement!

Providing effective feedback and securing an impact

Following an observation of their lesson, providing feedback to a colleague can take one of three routes. It can be:

1 Very positive for both parties: both professionals have had an input into the process, shared their views and come to an agreed judgement, planning the next steps for both the subject leader and teacher.

2 Neutral for both parties: there are no clear messages or action points which have emerged and the opportunity for professional development has been missed due to concerns over upsetting a colleague or simply not being interested in the chance to acknowledge good practice and to develop it further into the future or even transfer it to other colleagues.

3 Negative for both parties: there is no professional discussion and the judgement is delivered in the form of a lecture which is either passively accepted by the teacher, who takes no subsequent action and is not supported by the subject leader, or responded to negatively by the teacher so that the professional relationship breaks down.

It is a sad fact that the quality of feedback following an observation can vary greatly. Some schools have developed a firmly embedded culture of coaching, mentoring and professional feedback, whereas others are trying their best but lack direction. In extreme cases there are schools (an ever-decreasing number, thankfully) where observation is used negatively, to the detriment of the teacher involved. At the very least, if the opportunity for professional discussion between colleagues after an observation has been completed is managed incorrectly, then a considerable amount of very valuable time has been wasted.

To make the most of the opportunity, professionals should aim to follow these basic principles and procedures:

● Arrange the feedback, at a mutually convenient time, as soon as possible after the observation. Ensure that you have had time to reflect on the lesson, making any necessary notes or completing any standard feedback records required by your school. It is also important to consider your colleague, who might be very nervous about the feedback and so would prefer to have the discussion sooner, rather than later. Try to meet within three days at most but ideally within the next 24 hours.

● Allow sufficient time for the feedback. You want to foster a professional dialogue and that can take time. It is best to conduct this meeting after the school day, in a quiet space where you won't be interrupted. Avoid break times or lunch times, during which teachers will often need to prepare subsequent lessons – or actually have a break!

● Be clear about the messages you wish to give the teacher. If necessary, discuss your findings and initial judgements with a senior colleague or line manager. They will commit the time if they genuinely support the use of lesson observation as a form of professional development. You should also make careful use of language. If your school has chosen to use OFSTED evaluative language such as 'outsanding', 'good', 'satisfactory' and 'inadequate', then you must ensure that you use this language in the same spirit. Don't tell a colleague their lesson was 'good', if you then intend to talk through evidence which points towards a 'satisfactory' judgement.

- Be honest, specific and professional. Whether your feedback is positive or negative, you should be direct and not attempt to dilute the message you are giving. Often teachers will ignore positive feedback and only focus on the negative – therefore it is important to ensure that your praise is as clear as the more negative aspects of the discussion, should there be any. It is also important to make use of specific examples and evidence from the observation, which you can cross-reference with the agreed criteria for the lesson observation. In doing so, it is possible to avoid your colleague feeling that you are making a personal judgement about their teaching and instead focus on your comments about the professional aspects of their role.

- If you are delivering a negative message, remember to talk about the individual's capacity to develop and improve. They should not feel that you are making a judgement which they will be left to address on their own, whilst you walk away. You should consider any points for development as points for you *and* the teacher to work on. For example, it may be necessary for you to provide follow-up support in the form of additional training, team teaching or a short-term action plan. You are there to make a judgement and then provide support.

- If necessary, give your colleague the opportunity to prove themselves or to share their expertise. If you have highlighted areas for improvement then you should arrange a follow-up observation in which the teacher can demonstrate their improvement, and have it formally acknowledged. On the other hand, if you have found some excellent classroom/subject practice in a teacher, then arrange (with their consent) for other colleagues to observe this practice as a way of sharing their skills.

 example

Using lesson observation and feedback to improve the quality of provision for pupils in the school

Jane was a recently appointed subject leader for Design and Technology (DT). To help address her need to develop her understanding of the standards of teaching and learning across the school, she scheduled a number of lesson observations covering the different age groups within the school. She already felt confident in the overall DT curriculum for the school as a whole, but prior to each observation she made sure to review the school curriculum map, in line with the teacher's planning.

Having completed the majority of her observations, where her judgements had all been that teaching and learning was at least good and in some respects outstanding, she conducted her final observation, in which she saw that there were significant teaching and learning issues.

Having completed the observation, she then used the wide range of evidence she gathered, which included observations of specific pupils and notes of their comments, to make an initial overall judgement of inadequate teaching and learning. Having made this cursory decision, she then used national subject association websites and returned to the national curriculum guidance to exemplify the standards that the children in this specific year group should be achieving, compared to what was evident in the lesson. In doing so, she began to see that the main issue was down to inaccurate and insufficiently challenging teaching. This had resulted in the children not developing their designing skills and lacking any development in their use of different joining techniques because of their poor understanding of the materials on offer to them.

Jane was confident in her subject knowledge but was a little unsure about her judgement, wanting reassurance as the teacher in question was also a senior teacher within the school. She therefore discussed her findings confidentially with his line manager, who concurred with her findings and also provided some advice on how best to address the issue with her colleague.

Jane then met with the teacher she had observed, doing so after school on the same day as the observation. Having talked through her findings and presented the evidence, the teacher could not dispute the judgement that Jane had made about the lesson but he was very upset that this formal judgement had been made when he was clearly just having an 'off-day' and that his reputation would now be sullied. Jane reassured him that this was not a final, damning judgement but a snapshot of events on a particular day which she would be happy to support him in developing. However, at the same time, Jane also made it clear that this would have also been the judgement that any external body, such as OFSTED or the local authority, would have made, had they conducted the observation. Hence, it was better for the teacher that Jane had picked up on the issues and was now able to provide support.

By the end of the feedback meeting, Jane and the teacher had drawn up a short-term action plan for improvement which clearly stated actions and success criteria for both parties. Jane committed to providing additional support in the form of collaborative planning and team teaching, and the teacher committed to visit other colleagues to observe their practice, as well as participating in some local authority subject training. It was also noted in the action plan that Jane would complete a follow-up observation in six weeks' time, which would focus on the issues raised in the first observation.

By the time of the follow-up observation, Jane and the teacher had completed all their agreed actions and had developed an excellent professional relationship in which the teacher felt able to discuss his needs and used Jane as a form of continuing professional support. The outcome of the observation was that the teaching and learning was now deemed to ▷

be good with outstanding elements, with significant development in the areas of designing and making.

In the second feedback meeting, the teacher apologised for his initial anger at the previous judgement and thanked Jane for her support. He admitted that he had actually been struggling with aspects of the DT curriculum for some time, but had not previously felt able to express his concerns. The meeting was concluded with a further commitment for Jane to conduct another observation in 12 weeks' time, as a 'top-up' professional development opportunity, at the request of the teacher.

Overall, it is important to remember that as subject leaders we must maintain our focus on securing the best learning experiences for the pupils in our schools and that lesson observation is one highly effective means of establishing the specific curriculum strengths and areas for development within each of our staff. As long as the focus remains on lesson observation as a form of monitoring, evaluation *and* continuing professional development then, though it may prove uncomfortable at times, we can all benefit from the process.

 **brilliant** recap

The four most important messages from this chapter for the Brilliant Subject Leader are:

1   Prepare yourself and your colleagues for observations: establish ground rules, protocols and expectations which are shared and mutually agreed.

2   You are observing the lesson to make a professional judgement against given criteria: don't get personal – we all have different teaching styles and different isn't necessarily wrong. Keep focused on the basic principles of effective teaching and learning.

3   Be confident in your judgements but remember that confidence comes from having all the facts. Gather as much information as possible to be sure that your judgement is accurate.

4   Remember that you and the teacher being observed are working in partnership rather than in opposition. You both want the same goal – effective teaching and learning. There may be uncomfortable periods and emotions may run high but if you balance the professional challenge with professional support, there will ultimately be improvement.

CHAPTER 5

Pupil voice

A s you travel deeper into the undiscovered country that is subject leadership, it is easy to find yourself surrounded by a jungle of paperwork which can make you feel that you have ventured too far from the chalk-face and that there is a need to return to our professional compass – i.e. ensuring the best opportunities for the children in our care. Pupil interviews are one of the most powerful forms of subject leader monitoring and evaluation, due to the simple fact that it is an opportunity to talk directly to and take feedback from the ultimate focus of our job – the children!

As professionals, we regularly make decisions about the provision in our schools, such as the structure of the curriculum, the resources we need and the broader learning environment. These decisions are usually made with the best of intentions, based on tried and tested practice, professional research and well-founded educational principles. However, it is important to remember that there are times when such decisions should be informed by and made in conjunction with the children in the school, rather than subject leaders and senior staff doing so on behalf of their pupils. There have been many occasions in the past when, as a class teacher, I have spent a long time devising what I considered to be an innovative and inspiring means of learning a new concept or a more stimulating way of structuring a lesson, only for the pupils to completely take the wind out of my educational sails by either failing to connect with the learning or by pointing out that there is another simpler and more effective mode of learning that they would have chosen.

Furthermore, the pupils in your school will always provide you with honest and direct feedback about the experiences and opportunities you have provided for them in your role as a class teacher and/or subject leader. There have been occasions when I have felt that a new initiative has been either a resounding success or an undeniable failure, when in actual fact the feedback from the pupils provided a different viewpoint which I had been unable to appreciate in isolation. The children will naturally evaluate such experiences and share this without the baggage of professional ego, staffroom politics and government agenda that can sometimes cloud our own judgement.

As we strive to continually follow the mantra of *working smarter, not harder* in all aspects of our role as subject leaders, then it makes sense for us to utilise

utilise the power of the pupil voice

the power of the pupil voice – the opinions, insights and perspectives that will be freely and openly offered by the children in our schools, whenever we make any significant decisions about aspects of the curriculum which directly impact on their learning.

As a new subject leader, pupil interviews can seem like one of the more amorphous forms of monitoring and evaluation. They can take many different forms, in order to meet the many different needs of your leadership role, as well as varying greatly depending on your individual school context. Therefore, the remainder of this chapter will be dedicated to providing you with some models of how pupil interviews might be used, the information that can be gained from them and the actions you might take as a result.

The key to making effective use of pupil interviews, as with any monitoring and evaluation, is to use them only when it is meaningful to do so (i.e. related to or within the realm of experience of the children) and to maintain a very clear purpose for doing so, which supports you in further developing your knowledge, understanding and skills as a subject leader.

Pupil interview checklist

The specific arrangements for pupil interviews will vary between schools. Some may have a very clearly defined protocol for the process, whereas others may use the techniques only informally. However, there are some basic principles of any pupil interview that you should always carefully consider prior to starting the process. These include:

- **The age of your interviewees**: Will you be speaking to single-age group representatives or mixed-age group panels?

- **The ability of your interviewees**: Will the group comprise children of varying abilities or will you be speaking to children of similar abilities? How might this affect the way in which you phrase questions or take feedback?

- **Recording the interview**: Will you be making notes as the children speak? Are you planning to make an audio or video recording? How will this affect the dynamic of the group (some children become very self-conscious when being recorded)?

- **Structuring the 'interview'**: Will the interview be arranged as a simple panel/circle discussion, with questions being asked and responses offered? Will there be a focus to the interview, such as an activity or materials to review? Are you looking for verbal responses or the way in which the children react to a given situation or activity?

- **Questioning the interviewees**: Have you devised a list of key questions which will support you in making comparisons between different groups? How will you provide the children with the opportunity to fully express their opinions? Are you clear of your ground rules for discussion (no teacher/pupil names to be used; discussion to remain focused on questions, not personal issues between teacher and pupils or pupils and peers, etc.)?

- **Demography of the interviewees**: Do you need to consider the profile of the group beyond chronological age? For example, are you interested in establishing whether children with SEN have different opinions to the Gifted and Talented pupils? Is there parity of educational experience and support between looked-after children and other students? What are the opinions of the traveller children in the class/year group/school?

- **Timing and location of the interviews**: Do you have a suitably quiet place to conduct the interviews or are you planning for them to happen within the normal classroom setting (this relates to the focus of the interview)? Have you notified the teachers of your plans? Is there sufficient time available for you to hold a useful discussion?

- **Use of the results**: How are you going to make use of your findings? Will you provide written feedback to the teacher/s? If you have significant concerns, are you aware of whom to gain further advice and support from? How will you ensure that the time you have spent on the pupil interviews will have a positive impact on standards of teaching, learning and achievement?

 **brilliant** example

The impact of teacher–pupil feedback

Amal was a recently appointed English subject leader. The school data indicated that standards in writing had started to decline over the past three years. Whilst the decline was not dramatic, it needed to be investigated so that action could be taken to avoid any further decrease in standards.

Amal noted that over the past four years, there had been some significant staff changes and he was keen to establish whether there was consistency in approach to the teaching and learning of writing skills across the school. As part of this subject audit, he chose to focus on the quality and impact of teacher–pupil feedback.

In the early stages of his investigation, Amal collected samples of work from all teachers and chose to look at marking feedback and comments with the goals of gauging the consistency of approach across the school.

It became clear at this early stage that many of the staff had interpreted the school's marking policy in a variety of ways. Some staff were writing very detailed, possibly inappropriately complex, comments for each piece of work, whereas others were using only a marking code with limited additional written commentary. In most cases, marking and feedback appeared to be effective for many of the pupils, but it was less clear which of the approaches was *most* effective in terms of raising standards of writing.

Rather than trying to make such a significant decision alone, Amal chose to use pupil interviews to discuss the current marking practices with the pupils, in the hope that they would be able to provide some real-life commentary on how useful the teacher marking was for them, on an individual basis.

Amal chose to speak to a cross-section of pupils in each year group, including differing abilities, varying degrees of SEN and a balance of genders. The findings of the pupil interviews were very revealing and indicated a clear direction for Amal. The findings are summarised below:

- Pupils rarely read any feedback which was more than two or three lines in length.
- Some individuals reported that they often ignored written feedback completely, in favour of scanning the work for indications of rewards/ merits in line with the whole school/subject reward system.

▶

- Some pupils were clear about the general aspects of their writing that they needed to improve, but were much less sure of what they had achieved in each piece of writing.

- The majority of pupils felt that they benefited most from teacher marking/feedback when there was the opportunity to discuss this in person.

Amal then decided to share this feedback with his colleagues through a subject-focused staff meeting. Some were surprised by the pupils' responses, as it was clear that what some colleagues felt was good practice was not necessarily perceived as such by the pupils. It was also interesting that all the staff commented that, on reflection, they were often too 'negative' in their marking – focusing too heavily on 'next steps', rather than achieving a balance between positive comments and areas for improvement.

As part of the staff meeting, Amal then led his colleagues to review the marking policy in order to devise a consistent approach to marking which would be effective in supporting the development of writing for the majority of pupils. The outcome was that they would trial a system of 'highlighted' marking. The proposed marking system involved:

- Two different colours being used to highlight/mark work consistently across the school: blue (indicating achievement) and green (indicating next steps).

- Each marked piece of work would include a ratio of approximately two positive comments/blue highlights to every one next step/green highlight. These would be indicated within the body of the writing using the appropriate colour.

- At the end of the writing, the marking feedback would be summarised as a single, short sentence directly related to the appropriate highlighting colour.

- At the discretion of the teacher, there would be at least one session per week where the children were empowered with the time to review the teacher's feedback and to act on/follow up this marking within the session.

It was decided that the marking system would be trialled for a period of three weeks by all staff, after which time Amal would conduct another round of pupil interviews in conjunction with his own sampling of work, in order to evaluate the initial impact of the changes.

The outcomes were remarkable. When Amal repeated his interviews with the same cross-section of pupils he found that the children:

- were clearer about their successes;
- were more sharply focused on the specific areas/small steps which would lead to improvements in their writing;
- felt that their writing was valued by their teacher and their efforts were appreciated;
- valued the time that their teacher had committed to marking their work, as they felt it was helping them to improve;
- appreciated the opportunity to discuss the feedback with teachers, as it often helped to clarify exactly what they should do to continue to improve their writing.

Amal provided this feedback to his colleagues, who were all motivated by such a positive response. Some staff also provided examples of individual pupils who were now making enhanced progress as a direct result of more focused marking and quality feedback. In addition, some staff commented that they found this new approach to marking/feedback to be more manageable within their busy weekly schedules.

Choosing a focus for pupil interviews

As with any form of subject leader monitoring and evaluation, the use of pupil interviews must be carefully selected to ensure that your valuable time is used wisely to access relevant information which will help to improve achievement, attainment and the quality of provision in your subject. As your confidence grows in your leadership role, you will find your own effective and innovative uses of pupil interviews to support your role within the context of your school: however, it may be useful to share some specific examples of best practice in this area. Below, you will find some instances where empowering children to exercise their pupil voice, in the form of a pupil interview, can have a positive impact on your subject and enhance your effectiveness as a subject leader.

Purpose 1 – Learning vs doing

As teachers and subject leaders, we are all now focused on structuring lessons based on clear learning objectives, which are the component parts of a broader sequence of learning contributing to the development of new skills, knowledge and understanding. This is now so entrenched in our professional psyche that it can be easy to forget that these are skills we *acquired*; thinking in terms of learning objectives, success criteria and targets does not come naturally to the rest of the human race! It is therefore important that we regularly evaluate the learning in our schools and reflect on the degree to which our understanding and leadership of learning is being effectively communicated to the children in our care. To facilitate this, there is one simple but powerful opening question that can be asked of children of all ages: 'What are you learning?'

Depending on the age of the child, the learning ethos in the classroom and the way in which the teacher uses learning-related language, responses can vary greatly. When I have asked this question of pupils in the past I have received responses which have included:

- '... to finish these ten questions'
- '... to make my writing get to the bottom of the page'.

And, more encouragingly:

- '... to understand the feelings of others'
- '... to be better at using my times tables to solve problems'
- '... to not give up when I'm stuck with spelling'.

As is evident in these responses, there can be great variety in the way in which individual pupils interpret the term 'learning'. In cases where the understanding of learning is clouded, it can be useful to ask a follow-up question of: 'What are you doing and what are you learning – are these things different?'

I have always been amazed by the way in which the phrasing of a question can unlock understanding in young minds. In instances where pupils have been heavily focused on the completion of an activity or performing a particular task, which may have masked their understanding of the learning that is taking place, probing deeper with carefully chosen questions has helped me, as a subject leader, to judge the degree to which there is good quality learning taking place in a classroom. In some cases pupils have been able to very succinctly tell me that they are, for example, '... doing all these calculations to learn how to use an array for multiplication' whereas others have merely reported that they are '... doing the investiga-

> the phrasing of a question can unlock understanding in young minds

tion because Mrs X said we have to' without being able to relate this to learning or a deeper purpose. In the former case, it was clear to me that there was a well-established learning ethos in the classroom, where the pupils understood the purpose for their learning as being focused on developing their own abilities and skills rather than to mechanically meet the demands of the teacher, as was evident in the latter response.

From a subject leader's perspective, these kinds of questions can provide you with the start of a thread of investigation which can be followed up with further and more formalised monitoring and evaluation. For example, in the case of the child who could very clearly define the differences between, and interdependence of, learning and doing, I would be eager to explore how the class teacher had developed these higher-order skills with their pupils. As a subject leader, I would then seek to devise ways in which to share this effective practice with colleagues across the school. Alternatively, where discussions with an individual child or group of children had demonstrated little or no understanding of the learning taking place in the classroom, I would want to follow this up with the teacher to explore whether this is simply an issue isolated to one child/group, or whether there was a need for support and guidance for the teacher in developing a purposeful learning ethos in their classroom.

Overall, by asking these questions regularly and widely across the school you, as a subject leader, will begin to develop a 'feel' for learning in your subject which can then help to inform the focus of your future monitoring and evaluation.

brilliant tip

When arranging pupil interviews it is obviously good practice to inform staff of your plans prior to the discussions taking place. However, to get a 'real' view of the issue you are investigating, take time to select the children to interview yourself with input from the teacher. If the teacher is asked to select the children in isolation, they may choose the 'model' pupils, understandably following their natural instinct to provide children who will give a 'good' reflection of life in their classroom. By involving yourself in this process, you will be able to ensure that a genuinely representative cross-section of children is selected, and that the selection works well in conjunction with the demography of children selected from other year groups.

Purpose 2 – Triumph, tweak or transform?

As a subject leader, it is more than likely that you will be bombarded with a plethora of new initiatives, schemes, resources and potentially 'faddish' approaches to learning on a regular basis. One of the challenges of the role is how to filter the valuable educational practice from the educational detritus, in order to enhance the provision for your subject across the school, as well as developing the skills of the teachers in your subject and providing the best opportunities for the pupils. You need to decide whether you have *triumphed* as a school with an already effective approach empowering you to ignore external initiatives; need to *tweak* current practice to incorporate the most valuable aspects of new resources, initiatives and guidance; or whether there is an aspect of the subject which needs to be *transformed* through rigorous review and development because you have identified a significant weakness or opportunity for enhancement.

In some cases, decisions are made for you. These might be the result of financial constraints, such as a published scheme lacking sufficient value for money to warrant significant expenditure from your curriculum budget. You may find that national initiatives do not meet the needs or context of your school and would therefore be an ineffective use of leadership and curriculum time. Alternatively, there may simply be a more effective means of working already in place at your school, which would not be enhanced through new approaches.

> in some cases, decisions are made for you

Nonetheless, there will often be situations where the way forward is unclear and there may be many 'what-ifs' and 'maybes' surrounding your decision-making process. As a subject leader, you will be looked to as the person who will seek out the answers to the questions, explore the grey areas which emerge from discussions and come to a final decision for the subject or provide a recommendation to senior colleagues. It is at times like these that pupil interviews can prove invaluable.

In the case of a new curriculum planning scheme or resource, you would certainly wish to gain the opinions of the teaching staff that would be required to use them as a part of their daily, weekly or termly practice. However, as mentioned earlier, this will give you only part of a broader picture. By speaking to colleagues, you will obviously gain substantial professional insight, from a well-formed and valuable source, but it is only one of two important perspectives. We must remember that, whilst the teachers will be using the planning scheme or resource in their teaching, pupils will also be subject to learning within the context of the scheme or resource and therefore, their perspective is equally important.

In one situation, a Science subject leader was interested in purchasing an extensive range of published interactive whiteboard materials, which included animated models of investigations and videos to exemplify a variety of scientific processes. The intention was that these materials would be used to supplement the limited stock of practical investigative equipment and resources, over which the teaching staff regularly came into scheduling conflicts. When the materials were presented to the teachers, by the subject leader, there was significant interest and everyone could see the value in using these materials.

Following this, the subject leader then presented the same materials to a group of pupils who, whilst they liked the design and interactivity of the software, felt that they gained more from completing the investigations practically, as that helped the concepts to 'stick in [their] heads'. This was the first time that this particular perspective had been highlighted for the subject leader and, as a result, the decision was made to buy a limited number of the interactive whiteboard materials, focusing on the more abstract scientific concepts, whilst the remaining budget was spent on purchasing further practical investigative equipment to support children in carrying out their own scientific experiments. In this situation, the subject leader chose to *tweak* the school's provision, rather than making a *transformational* decision which may have been counter-productive when viewed in conjunction with pupil opinions and perspectives.

Purpose 3 – Meaningful and motivated!

It is universally acknowledged that for effective learning to take place, all learners must understand and value the meaningful context for learning, which ideally draws parallels with their own cultural and social context, resulting in each individual being motivated to engage with learning. However, in some schools and for some individuals, the motivation to learn can be the biggest barrier within the classroom. As a subject leader, you need to ensure that all children are provided with meaningful and motivating contexts within which to learn.

In order to ensure this, you may wish to make use of pupil interviews in order to gauge the degree of pupil motivation and interest within your subject. Your discussions might focus on occasions when children have most enjoyed learning in the subject. This could also equate to what they consider to be their most memorable learning experience. Some examples from my own investigations have included opportunities for practical or hands-on learning, experts who have visited the school to demonstrate the 'real-life' application of school skills, or occasions when the children have taken the lead on how learning should be structured or demonstrated. Such discussions would then provide you with information which, when combined with teacher assessment and professional reflection, helps you to develop a profile of effective learning in the subject, within your school.

> gauge the degree of pupil motivation and interest within your subject

Using this profile as a guide, it would then be possible to work with colleagues to review planning, as detailed in earlier chapters, to ensure that teaching and learning is structured in the most appropriate manner for the school and the pupils it serves, to result in motivating and meaningful learning experiences for all. It would then also be interesting to conduct a follow-up pupil interview, after there has been sufficient opportunity for you and your colleagues to implement any structural changes or content revisions, in order to evaluate the impact of recent developments. Are the children now more motivated than previously? Are they able to recount memorable learning experiences with greater alacrity?

Other useful key questions

In addition to the examples above, I have also detailed some individual questions which you might choose to use during pupil interviews. These questions have been used with children in Upper Key Stage 2 and above, as they are presented here. When using these questions with younger children, it would still be important to investigate the content of these questions; however, you would need to carefully frame the question to meet the level of understanding of the child. For example, when discussing progress and targets, a subject leader may choose to use the 'two stars and a wish' approach, which is commonplace in many schools. You could therefore frame this question within the context of the child naming the two aspects of the subject they see as their 'stars' (their best bits!) and one area where they would 'wish' to improve. In these situations, remember that you are also a teacher! Use your skills in communicating with children and developing a rapport with the youngest learners to benefit you as a subject leader.

● What have you learnt about [this subject/aspect of the curriculum]?

● How have your skills improved in [this subject/aspect of the curriculum]?

● In which areas do you feel you made good progress and why?

● What difficulties do you have and what are you and/or your teacher doing to overcome them?

- Are you given regular and useful feedback on your progress?
- Do you feel you can ask for help when you need it?
- What or who helps you to learn and why?
- Is there anything that hinders your learning and why?
- What do you feel is your next target for learning in this subject and why?
- What other support do you think you might need to progress and develop?
- What do you enjoy the most about this subject? Why?

To reiterate, these questions must be used with care and selected in relation to your chosen purpose for the pupil interview.

Pupil interviews and work scrutiny

In some schools, pupil interviews and work scrutiny may be viewed as two entirely separate processes, completed for two different purposes. In such situations, work scrutiny is often solely focused on issues such as quality/consistency of presentation; quality of teacher marking and feedback; indicative levels of attainment across the school in the subject and consistency of teaching and learning. These are all worthwhile foci for subject leader monitoring and evaluation, providing subject leaders and colleagues with a useful insight into aspects of the subject and performance of groups of children and specific individuals.

However, if the sampling and evaluation of pupil work is combined with a discussion between the subject leader and the pupil/s, then we can

> we can be *working smarter, not harder*

again be *working smarter, not harder*. For example, should you wish to gain a better understanding of how effectively colleagues are incorporating the principles of assessment for learning into teaching and learning in your subject, a combination of work scrutiny and pupil interviews can be very revealing. You would be able to discuss selected pieces of work with an individual child, helping you to gain a clearer understanding of the learning and support that has contributed to the finished piece of work rather than simply the quality of the final outcome. In many cases, the piece of work produced in the pupil's book, the finished DT product or the displayed art work may not reflect 'standardised' examples of levelled work in that subject, taken from national studies or sampling. Nonetheless, that individual may have worked with determination and vigour over an extended period, receiving personalised support from the teacher and support staff, progressing rapidly in comparison to their starting points and gaining a considerable sense of satisfaction from the end result. Therefore, whilst it may be less time-consuming to collect samples of work or whole books from teachers and then sit in a quiet space, reviewing each piece and making summary judgements, you must consider the validity of this isolated judgement. In the example detailed above, the same subject leader could easily reach two very different judgements above the learning in the classroom. When working without pupil input, the subject leader may perceive issues with the quality of provision in a class or year group and the rate of progress/skills development; whereas with the input of the child, the subject leader may develop a broader view of the quality of teaching, learning and provision in that class or year group as being a strength due to the journey that the child has taken in collaboration with the adults around him/her.

As previously discussed, it is essential that subject leaders gather as much information as possible before making any form of judgement. Develop a clear, rigorous and robust evidence base and then you will be more likely to draw accurate and meaningful conclusions which will support you in your role, leading to continuous subject development and improvement.

 **brilliant** timesaver

Regardless of the specific subject you lead, there will be an expectation for you to ensure that ICT is used to appropriately support teaching and learning within the context of your leadership role. As most, if not all, schools now have some kind of intranet, shared curriculum/staff school network/server or learning platform, why not use it to your advantage? Occasionally ask your colleagues to provide, where appropriate, electronic examples of pupils' work in which children have employed ICT to support teaching and learning. This is an efficient means by which to access and view samples of work, and you will also be developing an electronic portfolio of work, evidencing how ICT is used in your curriculum area.

brilliant recap

The four most important messages from this chapter for the Brilliant Subject Leader are:

1 Only use pupil interviews when it is appropriate to do so. Ask yourself whether the information you hope to gain from the pupils will help in your specific investigation and/or your broader leadership of the subject.

2 Choose your interviewees carefully. Are you investigating a broad subject issue, which requires a general cross-section of pupils, or are you looking at provision for a specific group?

3 Combine pupil interviews and work sampling, where possible. You will gain a more accurate insight into learning in your subject by talking to the individuals involved in it on a daily basis, thus melding two forms of monitoring and evaluation.

▶

4   Pupil interviews provide you with *one* perspective about an issue or aspect of your subject. Remember to combine this with the input of your colleagues, before making any judgements or significant decisions.

CHAPTER 6

Pupil tracking and data analysis

Over the past ten years the importance and relevance of assessment data in schools has grown significantly. At one time, the use of this information was the sole remit of the assessment leader, who would sit in his/her isolated tower of statistics, pouring over percentages and charts, performing the unique alchemy that is assessment analysis. The results of their secluded toiling would then be shared with the headteacher and school leadership team; in some cases a representative of the governing body might have been included. However, the use of this information was restricted to this select group. The headteacher would take the emerging priorities to possibly form an aspect of the school development plan; the leadership team may have taken some key messages from the analysis to guide their line management of staff; and the governor may have reported back the basic 'facts' of the school's data to other members of the governing body.

It is also an unfortunate fact that much of this analysis was completed retrospectively, with key staff reading and telling the 'story' of the school assessment data at the end of the academic year, rather than being central and influential characters who interacted with the development of the expansive narrative that is whole school assessment. This approach allowed only for comment on the historic data over the year, rather than encouraging positive and decisive action to secure improvement *within* the year.

Thankfully, the drawbridge of the assessment leader's castle has finally been lowered. In many schools there is now a palpable desire for assessment to be used dynamically by all relevant staff, with the overarching goal of securing the best outcomes for the children in our care, by ensuring the most effective journey for those same children through their education. However, even though the walls of the assessment castle are now filled with interested and dynamic individuals, enthusiastically picking through the colourful marketplace of pupil tracking and assessment analysis to find those valuable nuggets of information, many of those involved speak very different professional languages. You, as a new subject leader, may feel that you have just arrived at the gateway to the assessment castle, but that everyone inside seems to speak in a strange, mysterious dialect with foreign terminology you are yet to encounter.

> availability of data will vary between subjects

It is also important to note that the availability of data will vary between subjects. Given their higher profile within the national curriculum, subjects such as English, Mathematics and Science are often awash with different sources of assessment data and analysis, whereas assessments in subjects such as Art and Design, Music and Religious Education are often less prevalent.

The purpose of this chapter is to help you to find your way through the multifaceted world of assessment, in the most efficient way possible, to ensure that you are again empowered to *work smarter, not harder*!

Attainment and achievement

Before delving into the depths of whole school assessment and pupil tracking, it is important to develop a shared understanding of the difference between *attainment* and *achievement*. As a subject leader, you will regularly encounter these two terms, often used in common parlance as a matching pair – a celebrity couple in the world of assessment in the same vein as 'Posh and Becks' or 'Mickey and Minnie'. In actual fact, it is essential to understand these two terms as markedly different. It can be helpful to make the distinction between attainment and achievement thus:

● Attainment is a formal, standardised measure of a child's performance, against national levels. It is essentially based on the sampling of a child's ability at a particular point in their education. Attainment is most commonly and contentiously measured through testing; however, there are also new emerging approaches such as Assessing Pupils' Progress (APP) which, whilst supporting continuous teacher assessment, also provides teachers and the SLT with information relating to attainment.

● Achievement also relies on judgements being made about a child's academic development; however, it takes into account the starting point of the individual when measuring achievement. This starting point is compared with a significant 'end' point, which may be the end of a term or academic year, and the amount of progress that child has made is measured. It is then possible to assess whether the child has made appropriate progress, based on their starting point, which indicates the quality of achievement. When this analysis is scaled up from the individual child, to cohorts, key stages and the whole school it can form a detailed picture of how effective the provision is within the school. Again, one more recent form of assessment which supports the tracking of a child's achievement is APP. This will be discussed later in the chapter.

Assessment *of* learning and assessment *for* learning

When making distinctions such as those above, it is important to remember that both attainment and achievement are assessments *of* learning, rather than assessment *for* learning. As a subject leader, one aspect of your role would be to focus on the effective use of assessment *for* learning within your subject area. As mentioned in previous chapters, this would include the effective use of teacher–pupil feedback through marking and target setting, evaluated by lesson observation, work scrutiny and discussions with pupils. You would seek to establish the degree to which teachers are successfully assessing, communicating and addressing the next steps in an individual child's learning.

The purpose of assessment *of* learning, as a tool for subject leaders, is primarily more strategic. Through the evaluation of assessment data across the school, focusing on the progress the pupils have made in relation to their starting points and the levels they have attained over a significant period, it is possible to gain an insight into the quality of the school's curriculum provision, teaching and learning. As a subject leader, you would hope to use effective tracking of pupil progress and assessment analysis to further develop your understanding of your subject and to help direct your future efforts to secure high standards and continuous improvement in your subject.

The subject-related data that is available to you as a subject leader will vary from school to school to a certain extent. There are many local authorities which promote a standardised approach to assessment analysis through the use of software, such as customised spreadsheets. On the other hand, some schools may well have devised their own methodologies and processes for data collation and analysis. In your

you may have the vision to implement your own approach

leadership role, you may have the vision to implement your own approach to tracking and analysing pupil data.

The specific approach is not necessarily relevant, provided that the analyses that are produced as a result are informative, valuable and accurate.

What should I be looking for?

As a subject leader, there are some specific aspects of the assessment data and related analysis for your subject that it is important to explore. These are detailed below.

Performance of pupils across the current academic year

As mentioned earlier, in the past the established convention in many schools was to review the attainment and achievement of their pupils at the end of the academic year. This would often be the first point at which any data had been formally analysed since the start of the academic year. However, it is true that this approach would often give school leaders a detailed and comprehensive view of what happened within the year, highlighting specific areas of success and weakness across many subject areas. It is also important to note that this approach seriously inhibits subject leaders and senior school leaders from having a significant impact on the quality of provision. It may be the case that priorities which emerge from the data analysis can be carried forward into the next academic year; for example, the 2009–10 data analysis might highlight Mathematics attainment as falling and addressing this could then become a focus for the 2010–11 academic year.

However, as school leaders are we being effective in our leadership of learning if we react to significant issues only in hindsight? Wouldn't it be better practice and ultimately more beneficial to the children in our care for us to try to identify these issues within the same year? At least then it would be possible for an effective subject leader to take decisive action to address emerging priorities before they become serious concerns that impede the educational development of large groups of children. This is why regular, within-year data analysis is central to effective leadership of a subject area.

Performance of different groups across the school

Nationally, there has been a growing emphasis on schools monitoring and evaluating the attainment and achievement of groups considered to be vulnerable to underachievement. Traditionally, these groups have included:

- children for whom English is an additional language (EAL);
- children with varying degrees of special needs (SEN);
- children who show significantly higher than average skill or aptitude in specific subjects (Gifted and Talented/GAT);
- children from a variety of different ethnic minority backgrounds;
- children in the care of child welfare services (looked-after children);
- children eligible for free school meals (FSM);
- traveller children.

However, as a subject leader, it can be helpful to look beyond these established groups to focus on a range of different analyses that will actually help to inform you, as a leader, within your particular school/subject context. These additional group analyses might include:

- **Gender**.
- **Term of birth**: For example, are those pupils within a cohort born in the summer term performing in line with their autumn-born peers?

- **Date of entry to the school**: For example, in some areas of high social mobility, a child might join a school partway through a key stage or year group. Do they progress at the same rate as those pupils who have had a more stable academic journey?

- **Military or civilian background**: In schools which serve a proportion of military families there will need to be analyses of the performance of pupils from both these groups to ensure that they are progressing at comparable rates, especially for the military pupils who might experience some turbulence in their education.

- **Tutor groups/year groups**: As a subject leader, this form of analysis will contribute to the identification of any specific issues within the teaching and learning across the school.

- **Involvement with intervention and support programmes**: Within some subjects, teachers and subject leaders may offer additional support for those pupils who, whilst they may not have a legally defined special need, may require short-term academic intervention. Is the intervention working? Are the gaps being closed effectively and efficiently?

Trends over time

It can be all too easy to focus considerable time and energy into the analysis of school and pupil level data in your subject for the current academic year, whilst losing sight of the bigger picture. As a subject leader, it is imperative that the data analysis for the current academic year is viewed in conjunction with the same types of analysis for the previous two to three academic years. This is important as, for example, whilst a slight variation between the performance of boys and girls in a particular year in a particular subject might be disregarded as insignificant, a more worrying trend might appear when viewed alongside historic data. It may become apparent that boys have consistently out-performed girls for the last three years, without any action having been taken; or there may be a steady drop in the performance of boys. All such issues would only be revealed and addressed through the comparison of data over an extended period. Doing so helps to ensure that you have a significant impact as a subject leader.

National and local authority data

In some subjects, such as English and Mathematics, it is usually possible to access comparative data for your school and those similar schools at a local and national level. This can be a helpful process because, though you may have a fully comprehensive analysis of the standards in your subject for your school, how do you know if these standards are appropriately high? By looking at the school data alongside national and local data, it is possible to identify a benchmark of good academic performance, against which you can judge the standing of your subject. If it appears that the school is below national and local averages, in the subject as a whole, or in specific groups as mentioned above, then this may warrant further monitoring and evaluation. Equally, where school data appears to exceed local and national trends, then this should be acknowledged and celebrated within the school and should support you as a subject leader in further developing the provision within the subject.

> identify a benchmark of good academic performance

Where can I find the assessment information I need?

As mentioned previously, there are a variety of different sources of assessment information which will vary greatly depending on the subject that you lead. For the purposes of clarifying the differing availability and sources of information it is helpful to use the core and foundation subject groupings. For our purposes, core subjects will be considered as English, Mathematics and Science (Science's inclusion being a point of contention for many), with the foundation subjects representing the remaining broad spectrum of subjects, including the Arts, Humanities, Modern Foreign Languages, etc.

Sources of assessment data for the core subjects

As a core subject leader, you are blessed with a wealth of assessment information, in various different forms. Whilst this means that you are fortunately knowledge-rich, it can sometimes feel quite challenging to new subject leaders because you have a myriad of different sources to compile, comprehend and reconcile before you can arrive at your summary findings. Below is a list of some of the key sources of assessment data available to you, with a brief summary of how they might be used.

RAISEonline

- An annually generated report, focusing on English, Mathematics and Science, for the previous academic year – commonly released in the November of the new academic year.

- Compiled using data submitted by schools and drawn from national testing.

- Analyses the attainment of children at the end of each key stage.

- Analyses the progress made by children between key stages in the form of Contextual Value Added (CVA) calculations. This is a measure of school effectiveness through the amount of 'value' added to the progress of pupils and includes factors such as prior attainment, gender, levels of pupil mobility, deprivation and other contextual factors. This also allows for easy comparison of school results with those of other, similar schools.

- Analyses the achievement and attainment of pupils in different vulnerable groups (as mentioned earlier).
- Supports the identification of two- to five-year trends in data.
- Allows schools to enter their own annual pupil tracking data for children progressing through a key stage, rather than between key stages. For example, it is possible to enter QCDA optional SATs results into the system, from which the subject leader for English could then perform question-level analyses for all the pupils by test paper, looking for significant trends.
- The contents of the reports are openly available to local authority education teams, school improvement partners (SIPs) and OFSTED.

Fischer Family Trust (FFT)

- Data analyses provided by an independent, non-profit-making charity, associated with supporting educational development and improvement.
- Acts as a database of information for the school, again focusing on the outcomes of children at the end of key stages for the previous academic year, and commonly released early in the new academic year.
- Provides predicted targets for individual pupils at the end of a key stage, based on their prior attainment at the end of the previous key stage.
- Targets are presented in the form of 'percentage chances' of attaining a particular level, which are also interpreted into national curriculum levels.
- Schools can select different degrees of challenge within the target-setting process, with the recommendation that schools use the FFT D targets which, if achieved, would bring the school into the top 25 per cent of schools nationally.

- Acts as an early warning system for emerging trends within the data, both positive and negative. Data is annotated with an upwards or downwards arrow when it appears that there has been a slight increase or decrease in data.

- Highlights significant key messages within the data through the use of 'boxes'. A blue box surrounding a data set indicates a significant drop in attainment, below national averages, whereas a green box indicates attainment significantly above previous school and national data.

- Offers the FFTlive service, which is an online version which can be used to generate a broad range of different analyses, produce a variety of individual pupil targets and track the progress of children within a key stage. The online and interactive nature of this element of FFT also allows schools to 'drill down' through data to help in the diagnosis of the issues underlying significant trends within the data.

Local authority 'first rush' data analysis

- Many local authorities will take the end of key stage data submitted by their schools to produce an initial set of data analyses for each individual school.

- These analyses are often in advance of the RAISEonline report; however, the data included in such reports will not have been validated (i.e. the data has not yet been confirmed as wholly accurate).

- Allows schools to start to review historic trends, as well as the performance of different groups (commonly focused on gender and SEN profile).

School level data

- This will include teacher assessments at key points (as identified by each school; often three times a year) as well as as summary assessments at the end of the academic year.

- This might also include summative judgements on standards taken from work scrutiny completed by the subject leader.

- Assessing Pupils' Progress (APP) records. This is a nationally standardised approach to assessing children in English, Mathematics, Science and potentially ICT. It is also intended to support teachers in diagnosing the specific needs of each individual child, to support their continued progress and development. The assessments are carried out by class teachers, moderated collaboratively within the school and compared to national standards files to ensure consistency within schools and across the country.

brilliant timesaver

Data within your school is likely to be held in a variety of forms. However, there should be one central database of pupil tracking and analysis which may be compiled and coordinated by the assessment leader. It is important that you, as a core subject leader, have access to this database as it will prove more efficient than you trying to collate the data on your own. Don't be afraid to ask for it – remember that we are striving to *work smarter, not harder* and the assessment leader might even feel heartened that someone else is showing an interest in it!

Sources of assessment data for the foundation subjects

As a leader of a foundation subject, you may well find that the available assessment information is limited and, in some cases, not necessarily compiled in a readily accessible or efficient manner. This can often be due to the fact that the vast majority of these assessments are conducted and completed by the class teacher solely for their own records, with the goal of informing the planning for their class. However, it is nonetheless important that some assessment analysis and tracking is conducted to allow you, as leader of the subject, to ensure that the provision in your subject is of a sufficiently high standard and to help identify those areas in need of development. Whilst much of this information will sit with the teachers in your school, as described above, it is not necessarily the most effective use of your time to collect in all their assessment documentation. I am sure that the majority of schools have a consistent record-keeping system for this kind of information; however, they will usually be geared towards the teacher being able to use them as an ongoing assessment tool rather than a support for data analysis.

You may also find that each teacher has interpreted the practical use of these documents in their own individual manner which, whilst it may work effectively for them, may not be easily understood by colleagues.

Therefore, to continue to follow our *work smarter, not harder* mantra, foundation subject leaders need to think creatively about how to access this information in the most efficient way possible. Below are some suggestions of how this might be achieved.

Subject standards meetings

- Arrange a time for you to lead a short staff meeting focused on your subject.
- Prior to the meeting, request that each member of staff bring a small sample of work from the pupils in their class. These should be indicative of the range of abilities in the class and relate to the national curriculum level descriptors for the subject.
- Then use the meeting time itself to lead staff in formally assessing the samples of work against the national curriculum level descriptors, with colleagues moderating one another's judgements.

- Take the minuted records of this meeting as an indicator of the standards in your subject across the school, within which significant strengths and specific areas for development should be identified.

Work scrutiny

As mentioned in previous chapters, this form of enquiry can be a powerful and insightful tool for the subject leader.

- Again, use the national curriculum level descriptors to review samples of work from a range of abilities as an indicator of levels of attainment across the school. This could be completed as a follow-up to a subject standards meeting, in which you may have now narrowed your lines of enquiry.

- Keep a record of your judgements. This doesn't necessarily have to be endless photocopies of pupils' work placed into an additional folder to fill a shelf. The children's books themselves are your portfolios of evidence, so simply make a note of the child's name, the date of the work and the assessed level. This means that you have the relevant assessment information to hand and can locate the work again should you need to refer to it in the future. It also saves a few trees!

Lesson observation/observing learning

For those subjects where it is hard to capture evidence on paper, such as PE and to some extent PSHE and RE (which are often focused on discussion), seeing the learning yourself can help you to make a judgement on attainment and achievement.

- Ask to sit in on a PE session. During the session, select some pupils (in collaboration with the teacher) that you will closely observe for the duration of the lesson. Take a copy of the level descriptors with you and check off each element against the physical evidence you see or hear from the pupil.

- Repeat this with the same group of pupils across the year and you should hopefully see progress or, if not, be able to take action to ensure that the standards of attainment and achievement in the subject are appropriately high.

- Again, keep your record keeping simple and efficient. Note the date of the session, the pupils tracked and the assessment alongside these. If appropriate, include some digital photographs, video or audio recordings which capture the evidence for your judgements. Save these electronically and they will form a solid evidence trail to support for summary findings for your subject.

Comparison with local and national standards

As a foundation subject leader you will not necessarily have access to a ream of statistical comparisons for your subject and those similar schools at a local and national scale. However, there are alternative forms of support.

- How closely do you work with schools in your cluster? You could arrange to meet up with your subject leader colleagues in other schools, with each of you bringing along samples of work similar to those discussed earlier.

- Through the comparison of these work samples and the assessments, you should be able to gauge if your school is meeting similar standards to those of other schools in your area. If not, it also provides the perfect opportunity to network with colleagues who are experiencing greater success and utilise their expertise to support the development of the subject in your school. On the other hand, you may find yourself in the position of being able to offer support and advice to your colleagues.

- Some subjects, such as RE and Geography, will have national academic associations. These groups can often provide subject leaders with useful information about national standards, assessment moderation or exemplars of good practice based on their research into the specific subject area.

brilliant tip

If you are able to work collaboratively with colleagues from other schools in your cluster, you could create a shared subject standards resource. This could simply be a shared paper file of exemplar pupil work that is indicative of national curriculum levels in the subject. This could form a support document for colleagues across the cluster. Alternatively, if you have access to a shared learning platform or VLE (read more about this in Chapter 9) then why not create a shared electronic subject leader space where you can collaborate on assessment, moderation and tracking activities? Subject leadership enters cyberspace!

What should I do with the information I gather?

Whilst much of this chapter has focused on the kinds of assessment information which might prove useful to you as a new subject leader and how to locate it, we must not forget the most salient aspect of the subject leader's role: impact!

It might feel satisfying to some to be very 'busy' collecting and collating assessment data, analysing it to within an inch of its life and then carefully filing it away alongside other subject leader documentation. However, if the process ends at this stage, you really need to ask yourself a simple question – what is the point? You may well have been heavily involved with working on the data for an extended period, but if there is no subsequent impact on standards of teaching and learning, it will all have been in vain.

Hopefully, you are now well on your way to being a highly effective subject leader and a key component in the machine that is subject leadership is the effective use of assessment analysis. You need to ensure that any data tracking and analysis you have conducted, no matter how small or expansive, has a positive impact in your subject area. Some examples of how to achieve this include:

- Feeding back on your findings to individual colleagues, for whom the information could help to enhance or refocus the teaching and learning in their classroom. This feedback should be carefully constructed to ensure effective professional development and to maintain a supportive working relationship, following principles similar to those shared in Chapter 4.

- Summarising your assessment analysis for colleagues with specific responsibilities. This might include highlighting strengths or weaknesses in your subject for a year group leader, or providing feedback on the effectiveness of subject-specific intervention programmes for the Special Needs Co-ordinator/Inclusion Manager.

- Sharing your findings, as well as your planned actions in response to these, with the school leadership team and/or school improvement partner to contribute to the school's continuous cycle of self-evaluation.

- Using your findings as indicators of standards which warrant further investigation. You may, for example, notice a possible trend in the achievement of a particular vulnerable group but feel the need to clarify the situation through further investigation. This could then prompt you to conduct further pupil interviews, work scrutiny or lesson observations to gain a better understanding. These would form the basis for a clearly defined and comprehensive evidence trail, exemplifying how you have made effective use of assessment analysis as a trigger for further monitoring/evaluation, from which you could document the subsequent impact of your actions.

Beyond the use of the data you have gathered and analysed as a means to secure and monitor high standards in your subject area, the use of pupil assessment data can also be an effective means of 'informing' other interested stakeholders. For example, the governing body of your school has a legal obligation to oversee the quality of provision in the school. This responsibility is largely delegated to the headteacher and school leadership team; however, there will still be the requirement for a named governor to offer support and constructive challenge to their associated subject leader within the school. The term 'challenge' can have negative connotations but in this sense it should be wholly supportive. The governor should ask the evaluative questions about the subject which any stakeholder might ask, such as parents, the SIP or OFSTED inspection teams, and having this conversation, in a supportive environment, which requires you to communicate your detailed knowledge of subject standards across the school, can often help to clarify your own understanding of the subject's position within the broader school context. You might also find that your named governor has hidden talents or valuable contacts which support you in developing prioritised aspects of your subject.

 **example**

Using data analysis as a trigger for the development of boys' writing

Marie had been working as her school's Literacy subject leader for a number of years. She had a vast amount of experience in supporting colleagues to offer the best learning experiences to the children in their classrooms. However, she had no experience of working with or responding to the school's analysis of pupil data in English because the analysis of this data had always been the responsibility of the deputy head, and for all of Marie's time at the school the standards in English had been high. She was aware of the positive outcomes for children at the end of each key stage, as these were reported publicly, but had no knowledge of the academic journey those same children had taken through the school. She was clearly being effective in her monitoring and evaluation of teaching and learning, providing individual classroom support for teachers as necessary, but she had had no cause to look deeper into the story the English data told.

However, the headteacher and deputy had noticed a potential trend in the most recent data analysis indicating that the performance of older boys in the subject was falling behind that of their female peers. This prompted a discussion between Marie and the school leadership team, as they sought to develop a strategy to investigate the issue and devise an appropriate action plan, if they found that one was warranted.

The first step in the process for Marie was to gain a sound understanding of the school's data analysis, so that she could fully comprehend the concerns of the school leadership team. This was achieved through a number of meetings between Marie and the deputy head, in which they systematically reviewed the data collected to look for potential patterns. It was clear that there were some 'dips' in the attainment and achievement of boys as they progressed through the school, which for one cohort was becoming more significant year on year.

Having gained a clearer understanding of the concerns from the data analysis, Marie then chose to conduct some further analysis of her own. She based this on the optional testing that had been conducted with the children over the past two to three years, focusing most heavily on the cohort of boys which appeared to present falling standards. She conducted a question-level analysis of the papers completed by the children and found that the boys were consistently being out-performed by the girls in aspects such as the structure of their writing.

This clear evidence then prompted Marie to investigate how other schools, facing the same issues, had taken positive actions to rectify any falling attainment and achievement. As part of her investigations, Marie discovered the StoryMaker project, based on the work of Pie Corbett. In conversation with colleagues at other schools, Marie discovered that this approach to raising standards in writing through the structured development of speaking and listening skills had positively impacted on boys' engagement with writing.

Marie then presented her question-level data analysis to the school leadership team, along with her proposals for the implementation of the StoryMaker project within their school. The support she received was overwhelming. The school leadership team were the first colleagues to see the potential value and impact of the project. Following Marie's presentation of the data analysis and her planned actions, they were soon joined by the teaching and support staff in the school. She ensured that everyone understood the purpose of the writing project and had clearly seen the evidence for the need for this to take place.

Over a period of 18 months, Marie was involved in considerable professional development opportunities, for both herself and her colleagues, to ensure the effective implementation of the StoryMaker project. At the same time, she also focused the majority of her subject-leader monitoring and evaluation on the progress of the project, drawing on evidence from lesson observations, work scrutiny and pupil interviews.

Ultimately, she chose to take the lead on the annual analysis of the English data, working in collaboration with the deputy head. Marie now understood the importance of the data analysis in ensuring that she knew her subject 'inside out' and could therefore be confident that her actions, and those of her colleagues, were having a positive impact on teaching and learning. It transpired that even within the first year there had been a noticeable impact on the engagement of boys with writing as they moved through the school. This was particularly evident in the fact that the attainment of boys and girls in writing had already started to realign and the gender gap was closing.

 **brilliant** recap

The four most important messages from this chapter for the Brilliant Subject Leader are:

1 Only conduct data analyses that will be useful to you as a subject leader – be clear about the purpose before you start.

2 Drill down through the data. It is better to check for any issues within different vulnerable groups and prove that there aren't any, rather than assume everything is on track, only to allow underachievement to become embedded.

3 Be proactive in the use of your findings. Your time is too valuable to simply carry out paper exercises. Draw out your findings and then take action to ensure a positive impact within the school.

4 Share your understanding with colleagues: no subject leader should be an island. If there are worrying questions being raised by your data analysis, acknowledge them with the appropriate colleagues so that they can support you in taking action to investigate and address these.

CHAPTER 7

Strategic planning for improvement

During our initial teacher training, one of the key aspects to be developed is the ability to plan for effective teaching and learning. Hours are spent planning every last teaching point and interaction, until sometimes it feels like you should plan opportunities for eating and sleeping! However, the intensive development of this skill will have resulted in you internalising the basic principles of effective planning to the extent that now, as an established teacher, those skills are naturally part of your professional being.

As you move into subject leadership, you will undoubtedly find that, regardless of the phase you work in or the subject you lead, the ability to devise and follow an effective strategic improvement plan is of utmost importance. Take heart then that the considerable effort you have committed to developing your planning techniques in the early stages of your teaching career will also pay dividends as you move into subject leadership.

Why is strategic subject improvement planning important?

As with any task which is additional to our class teaching commitments, it is essential to be clear about the purpose of the activity and the benefits that allocating more of our precious time will bring. This is a good opportunity to return to our *work smarter, not harder* mantra, acknowledging that if strategic subject improvement planning (SSIP) is effective and carefully constructed then you will find that you are more effectively using your available subject leadership time, thus ensuring that you have a considerable impact on your subject across the school.

To put it simply, effective subject improvement planning has two main purposes:

1   To focus and direct your actions as a subject leader over the course of an academic year.
2   To inform others of your plans for subject improvement/ development and the progress you have made to date.

We should first consider how subject improvement planning can be used to support your own work as a subject leader. As has been discussed in previous chapters, the role of the subject leader is significant to school self-evaluation and continuing improvement. When reading around the topic of subject leadership, it is easy to be left with the impression that you are expected to have two full-time jobs – the class teacher and the subject leader. Much of the guidance available on the role of the subject leader will explore the responsibilities of the position in isolation, ignoring the real-life context of all subject leaders

> we are teachers with a full-time classroom commitment as well

– that we are teachers with a full-time classroom commitment as well! Hopefully, what you have read so far has helped you to understand how you can effectively manage both these roles but it is your strategic subject improvement planning which will ultimately help you to strike this balance for yourself, within the context of your own school.

It would be unreasonable of any school or individual subject leader to expect that all the key elements of the role can take place consistently and continuously across a school year. It is practically impossible for any subject leader to complete all key monitoring and evaluation activities at the same time, with the same frequency across the year. For example, could you really analyse the school data looking for trends; interview six or more pupils; observe a lesson with the feedback prepared for later and audit curriculum coverage in the two available hours of subject leadership release time that you might have banked over the term? I am hoping that you will immediately be thinking 'NO!'. Remember that we are *working smarter, not harder*: trying to complete numerous tasks in a limited time would definitely be *hard* work – but would it really be *smart* to try to do so?

Ultimately, the probable outcome would be that any subject leader who tried to complete such herculean tasks in a short space of time, will only be able to pay lip-service to their monitoring and evaluation. The resulting impact would most likely be limited and, hence, precious time will have been wasted by simply being busy. Equally, if a subject leader hopes merely that they will be able to fit all these activities into the year at some point but never formally maps out how this will be achieved, again the result is likely to be that the subject leader will have a very limited impact on teaching and learning across the school.

This is where the true strength of effective subject improvement planning emerges. If constructed in the right way, a subject improvement plan (also termed a subject development/action plan in some schools) essentially forms your subject leader timetable for the academic year. It is a way in which you can effectively plan in your key subject leadership tasks, spread across an academic year, in order to ensure that you have sufficient opportunity to conduct your monitoring and evaluation in a timely manner, as well as securing a positive impact from these actions.

For some subject leaders, particularly those leading sizeable core subjects such as English or Mathematics, the subject improvement plan can also support the strategic development of the subject in line with whole school priorities. You may find yourself facing an academic year during which, for reasons identified by you and the school leadership team, your subject is a high priority. This might well mean that in addition to completing the 'standardised' monitoring and evaluation tasks required of all subject leaders, you also need to lead a significant strategic development within the subject. For example, a subject leader could be asked to introduce a new approach to teaching in their subject or to implement the use of a new national framework. Again, the subject improvement plan could be instrumental in structuring the implementation of this strategy across the school at a pace that matches the requirements of the broader school development plan, as well as showing consideration of the time available to the subject leader, and taking the pace of implementation at a class/individual teacher level into account.

As mentioned above, a well constructed subject improvement plan can be a useful tool for communicating your planned actions and the progress you have made to date, with other interested parties. Usually, your subject improvement plan would be shared with and approved by the school leadership team. The process may have involved some input from the members of the school leadership team, but it is ultimately the subject leader's responsibility to develop the initial ideas/priorities into a fully rounded, workable plan.

> it is the subject leader's responsibility to develop the initial ideas

Once the plan has been devised and approved by the school leadership team, they may only have sight of this again at key points during the year. You will be expected to use the plan to effectively manage your own subject leadership time, ensuring that all the goals within the plan are met on schedule. It is common for schools to have standardised subject improvement plan review points in the year. This might involve you annotating your original plan, indicating which of your goals have been achieved in full, outlining how much progress has been made towards the remaining targets and any changes made to the plan due to emerging issues. The form this evaluation takes will vary from school to school, as will the frequency of the reviews; however, the use of the plan at this stage remains the same – communicating your achievements and future plans to the school leadership team to ensure they are fully informed of the development of your subject. Not only does this help the team to ensure that you are meeting the expectations of your role, but it is also an important vehicle for identifying any additional financial or professional support that you might need to effectively meet the requirements of the plan.

Your subject improvement plan can also be a useful means by which to engage your link governor. In most schools, members of the school's governing body are associated with particular curriculum areas. The intention of this process is that this individual governor is the direct liaison between you, as the subject leader, and the broader governing body. In recent years, the relationship between subject leader and link governor has changed significantly. Previously, the governor associated with your subject merely needed to be aware of the content of your subject improvement plan and how you were progressing with the planned actions. However, as the profile of school self-evaluation has been raised at all levels of the school community, the governing body are now expected to be actively involved in a dialogue with the school which supports but also challenges the professional practice of the staff. Though that is not to say that you should fear the visit from your link governor!

In their renewed role, link governors should no longer just be interested in 'how things are going' but instead should be asking evaluative questions drawn from the whole school and subject priorities, such as:

● What percentage of children are on track to meet their end-of-year targets?

● How are you, as a subject leader, ensuring that there is sufficient provision for children with special educational needs?

The purpose of such questions is not to check the quality of your performance as a subject leader (although there is an inherent level of accountability which requires subject leaders to know their subjects well). The link governor should be asking these questions in order to better support you in your role. For example, if you are trying to improve community links in relation to an aspect of your subject, then use the link governor's local contacts to enable you to more effectively meet your targets. Do they know a local citizen who may be able to offer some expertise or knowledge? Are they a member of a local community group who could help? Equally, the link governor will probably be held to account themselves, as they will be required to report back to the full governing body on the progress of your subject improvement plan and how they are involved.

brilliant tip

Often the easiest way to communicate the progress you have made with your subject improvement plan is to do so visually. The school leadership team and governors will have seen your detailed strategic plan at the start of the academic year, which comprehensively outlined targets and deadlines. Why not keep a copy of this plan on display (possibly in the staff room or your classroom) on which you can highlight each goal as you achieve it? You could even annotate it with sources of evidence or examples of impact of your actions. By working in this way across the year, you can easily show your achievement and progress. It will also help you when you are asked to evaluate your progress by the school leadership team, as you then simply need to summarise your highlights and annotations to date.

The relationship between link governor and subject leader really should be viewed as a partnership. There should be an established protocol that you, as the educational professional, are in the position to make the best decisions about the development of your subject (in collaboration with the school leadership team), with the link governor taking the role of your critical friend – offering support but also asking questions to encourage you to look more closely at aspects of the subject that you may not have previously considered. When there is a truly evaluative professional relationship between the link governor and subject leader, the resulting dialogue can provide excellent 'practice' for the kinds of conversations you might have when the inevitable visit from the OFSTED inspectors occurs.

 **brilliant** timesaver

Planning collaboratively

Do you and a colleague lead similar subjects? Geography/ History or Art/Design and Technology? In which case it might be worthwhile exploring whether your priorities are similar too. You might be able to support each other in collaboratively creating your plan and ultimately completing the key task, monitoring and evaluation. Two heads are *always* better than one!

What should I include in my strategic subject improvement plan?

Being asked to write your first subject improvement plan, encompassing an entire academic year (and in some cases beyond) can be a daunting prospect. However, as mentioned earlier, as a result of your years of experience in planning countless, good quality lessons, your teacher's brain comes pre-loaded with the skill set required to write a successful subject improvement plan.

It is interesting how many parallels can be found between your familiar lesson planning and the strategic planning required from a subject leader, as the table below demonstrates.

Lesson planning	Strategic subject improvement planning
Learning objective	Subject priority for development
Success criteria	Success criteria
Duration of the plan (one session a week or medium-term)	Timescale for improvement (a term, number of terms or year)
Teaching points	Tasks to secure improvement
Teaching resources	Resources required (money/time)
Plenary	Evaluation of impact

The principles detailed here constitute the fundamental foundations for any successful subject improvement plan, with each individual aspect contributing to the overall effectiveness of the plan.

At this stage, it may prove useful to explore each aspect in a little more depth, before viewing the elements as part of a large plan.

Subject priority for development

The length of a subject improvement plan can vary between schools and subjects; however, it is common to find that a detailed subject improvement plan will cover a range of different priorities for different purposes. In some cases, a subject leader will be 'given' some priorities to address by the school leadership team. These priorities might have emerged from a whole school issue or a recent national initiative. In addition to such priorities, there should also be scope for you in your role as subject leader to identify areas in need of development or improvement. These might have emerged from your own monitoring and evaluation activities; alternatively, this might be the first time you are taking on the mantle of a subject leader and may be inheriting the subject priorities from your predecessor. In the case of the latter, try to meet with the previous subject leader if at all possible to try to gain a clearer understanding of why these priorities were selected. It might be helpful to ask:

- What sources of evidence were the priorities based on?
- Why was this issue felt to be of importance?
- Has any work already been completed in this area?

When recording the priorities on your subject improvement plan, remember to make sure it is K.I.S.S-ED (Keep It Straightforward Simple and Evidenced). Essentially, you should be wording the priority so that it can be easily understood by anyone who might need to read it. It is also essential to consider, when choosing your wording, how progress towards and achievement of your chosen priority will be evidenced.

- Does it require a statistical measure?
- Is it focused on the hidden curriculum (the hidden curriculum includes those elements of a child's education which extend beyond pure academic development, such as social skills, attitudes to learning and their personal development).
- What changes would be evident in the subject/classroom/ planning?

Success criteria

As with lesson planning, your success criteria should directly relate back to your original priority and clearly state what will be evident when the priority has been met. Again, the success criteria might be measurable through the use of statistics or data analysis. Equally, the success criteria might be observed through changes in methodology or documentation. Keep this in mind and make a careful decision about your success criteria.

Remember that the completed plan will be shared with the school leadership team, staff, governors, OFSTED and, in some cases, parents. Whatever you set as your success criteria will be what some or all of these stakeholders will expect to see as your evidence of improvement.

Timescale for improvement

When planning your subject leadership activity for the year ahead, it can be easy to over- or under-estimate the progress you might make with your priorities. In the early stages of your plan, the timescales you set can only be based on your best professional estimate. Remember to take into consideration times in the school year which might interfere with your plans, factoring them into your timescales. For example, does your school have any significant disruptions to the timetable around Christmas? Will this affect your plans to conduct pupil interviews or work sampling?

> the timescales you set can only be based on your best professional estimate

It is also important to note that your subject improvement plan should be a working document. During the course of the year you may realise that you need to accelerate or delay some of the planned tasks, as a result of additional strengths or weaknesses emerging from the monitoring and evaluation you have already completed. Keep a note of this and change your timescales accordingly. By keeping a record of the changes and the reasons why, you will have sufficient evidence to justify changing the shared plan with the school leadership team and link governor at the agreed review points.

Tasks to secure improvement

When you have arrived at your key priorities, you need to consider what it is that you and other relevant individuals actually need to do, in order to successfully address these priorities. It can be useful to think of these tasks as the stepping stones that will take you from one side of the fast-flowing waters of a school year to the other.

It is important to think through these tasks methodically and practically; where possible, make links with the routine monitoring and evaluation that you need to do. For example, if you are working to raise the profile of a particular skill in your subject, then why not use lesson observations or pupil interviews to assess the standards in this area throughout the academic year? Not only will you be gathering evidence and important insights into a priority within your subject improvement plan, but you will be able to simultaneously monitor the quality of teaching and learning.

Another *work smarter, not harder* opportunity that you should be looking for when planning your tasks is the chance to collaborate with colleagues. Is there another subject leader in the school working on a similar priority? Could you make use of some of their monitoring and evaluation evidence for your own purposes? For example, it may be the case that the Geography subject leader is evaluating the quality of mapping skills in a particular year group. This could present an opportunity to collaborate with the PE subject leader, who might already be planning to observe the teaching and learning involved with an orienteering unit of work, as part of the outdoor and adventurous activities curriculum. The two colleagues could collaborate, share evidence and ultimately save a great deal of time!

Resources

It can be all too easy to plan a comprehensive series of tasks in order to meet the needs of your subject. However, these plans may not be feasible when you consider the potential time and costs involved. It is important to consider both aspects carefully:

- **Cost**: Consider the costs incurred for any additional release time you might need in school. Depending on your area, you could base your calculations on roughly £150 for half a day of supply cover. Also factor in the costs that might be incurred through the purchase of new resources or the attendance of you/your colleagues on training courses related to your subject priority. Be realistic about these costs and record them clearly on your plan. This will allow the school leadership team to review the financial requirements of the subject leaders in order to allocate the budget (within other financial constraints) to support the subject improvement plans.

● **Time**: There is a constant pressure on staff meeting availability within a school year, as at any one time there will be a range of different people wishing to gain access to the staff as a whole group. Again, record any staff meeting time you might need to allow the school leadership team to allocate the staff meeting sessions according to need. You might even find that, if your plan is addressing a whole school priority, your requests to work with the staff in a formal meeting situation are given precedence over other subject areas. Also, you might be able to collaboratively lead a staff meeting. For example, the Geography and History subject leaders could jointly plan and run a staff meeting focusing on the development of those skills common to both subjects, under the umbrella of Humanities; or the Art and Design/Technology subject leaders could work collaboratively on their cross-curricular skills development.

Evaluation of impact

It is important to actively use your plan throughout the year, noting progress and annotating the plan with any significant changes. This allows you to easily provide feedback on your progress to date to any interested parties.

However, this alone may not be sufficient. It is important to be able to provide evidence of your progress through the improvement plan, where possible, so keep copies of any supporting documentation (such as records of monitoring and evaluation) alongside your subject improvement plan. This makes the task for formally evaluating your plan much easier and less time-consuming. Each school will have slightly different procedures for this process: some expect written evaluations, others rely on the link governor to be involved in a formal meeting; and others link this process directly to standard performance management procedures.

Regardless of the established protocol in your school, you need to keep 'So what?' in your mind throughout the evaluation process. Just as we might provide a writing frame to young children, you can do the same for yourself when evaluating your progress. For example, if you record that you 'completed lesson observations in three classes', then ask yourself 'So what?' You should then be able to identify what you or colleagues have done as a result of the lesson observation which has had a positive impact on teaching and learning, as well as how this contributed towards achieving the priorities on the subject improvement plan.

brilliant dos and don'ts

Do

✔ Keep (your priorities) Straightforward, Simple and Evidenced (K.I.S.S-ED).

✔ Use your subject improvement plan as a working document, recording your progress and evidence base.

✔ Make use of the support offered by your link governor wisely and to the school's benefit.

Don't

✘ Forget to include potential costs, in terms of both finance and time.

✗   Be over-ambitious in your plans: be rigorous when choosing the
    tasks that you intend to undertake but don't underestimate the
    time that is needed to complete them effectively.

✗   Worry about changing timescales on your plan: just make sure
    that you have clearly evidenced reasons why this has been
    necessary and how it affects the remainder of the original plan.

What should my strategic subject improvement plan look like?

Having explored the different fundamental aspects of effective
subject improvement planning, your mind might now be turning
to the practicalities of actually completing your own (in some
cases first) subject plan. As mentioned previously, all schools
will follow the basic principles that we have already explored
but there is great variation in how these are actually structured
on the page. Opposite are two examples of formats that have
actually been used by schools. Both schools shared the same
principles but, due to the preferences of the headteacher and
school leadership team, chose to use different formats.

As you will see in both examples, the basic principles are virtually identical but the layout varies slightly and both were used
successfully by two very high performing schools. This exemplifies that it is the *content* of the subject improvement plan that is
vitally important rather than the format. As a subject leader, you
must certainly comply with established processes in your school
but certainly don't waste time playing around with column
spacing and font styles. It is a working document and should
be treated as such: by the end of the year it is likely that your
plan will have handwritten annotations, highlights and dramatic
adaptations. So don't waste time making it *look* effective; instead
invest your time in making sure that it *functions* effectively as a
subject improvement plan.

Key issue					
Priority				Impact on learning, progress and achievement	Monitoring
Action				Evaluation	
Tasks	Staff leading	Time-scale	Resources	Success criteria	Completed
Evaluation of impact					

Example subject improvement plan (1)

Subject improvement plan						
Subject:		Subject leader:				
Whole school/ subject priority	Salient development points	Staff involved	Cost/ additional support needed	Key dates	Goals (to be evidenced and/or measurable)	Progress monitored by:

Example subject improvement plan (2)

 **example**

Collaborative subject development planning

Below we consider two different approaches to collaborative subject development planning. The first explores the collaboration between Music, Art and DT subject leaders to meet shared priorities; the second examines how a History subject leader utilised a collaborative approach to guide their progress through their subject development planning.

Case Study 1: Music, Art and DT

As a whole school, the school leadership team had identified a need to further develop the extent to which the school engaged with the parents and the broader community, in order to more explicitly share the learning opportunities that their children were experiencing. At this time, the school was simultaneously examining how the role of the subject leader could be streamlined and made more effective.

Taking these two priorities into consideration, the school leadership team suggested that Helena, the Art subject leader, Greg, the Music subject leader, and Sadie, the DT subject leader, work together to collaboratively structure their approach to addressing their shared 'community' priority.

Each subject leader devised and maintained their own separate subject development plans. However, in the case of the priority to develop the engagement of parents they worked together to coordinate their plans. In short, they chose to organise a family learning event encouraging parents to come into school, along with their children, to experience a number of different workshops which would give them a flavour of the learning that regularly happened within the school.

The family learning workshops were to be held one evening after school, towards the end of the academic year. The subject development plan devised by the group of subject leaders detailed an extensive period of preparation and planning for the event. For example, Helena, Greg and Sadie realised that running such an event, inviting all children to bring at least one additional family member, could have resource implications with potential financial repercussions. Fortunately, by pre-empting their financial requirements early in the academic year, they were granted additional curriculum funding to purchase materials for Art/DT workshops and to secure the services of the specialist music teacher beyond the conventional school day. Within the collaborative subject development plan, the subject leaders also set deadlines for key communications to be distributed to parents, ensuring that they avoided any clashes with 'busy' periods of the year for administrative staff.

An additional benefit of working collaboratively for these subject leaders was it raised their colleagues' awareness of the project. Again, as the plan was developed early in the academic year and was shared with their colleagues, they found that many staff volunteered their time to help run the workshops during the evening event. In this way, the plan was a useful tool as Helena, Greg and Sadie could delegate specific aspects of the preparation for the event to their colleagues, easing the considerable pressure of overseeing the project coordination. By the time the event was actually staged, the three subject leaders had arranged workshops spanning all their curriculum areas. These included making moving vehicles from wood and mechanical components; designing and making 3D sculptures; glass-making with a professional artist; a drumming workshop; a family orchestra with children conducting and pizza-making with a great variety of toppings!

Ultimately the event was a great success. Over 80 per cent of families were represented at the workshops: a significant increase in attendance when compared to previous 'single-subject' events which often only attracted 10 or 12 people out of a school community of over 200. The subject leaders reported a great sense of community across the school during the workshops: children were often able to lead their parents through the learning process as they were all based on actual learning that had taken place in the school, during the course of the academic year. In many cases, parents established new relationships with school staff and, in turn, the school staff gained some interesting perspectives on the children within the school. The three subject leaders were able to feedback on the success of the project, including their initial planning and preparation, to the school leadership team. It was subsequently decided that this model of collaborative planning for community events, linked to learning within the school, would be continued into the next academic year; this time focusing on Science, History and Geography.

Case Study 2

James had been leading Geography for a number of years and felt confident that the school's established curriculum structure for the subject was a particular strength, incorporating all the elements of the national curriculum, whilst also reflecting the particular interests and context of the school community, such as international links to partner schools. However, recently James had become increasingly concerned about the quality of assessment in the subject, across all year groups. This concern stemmed from the fact that the school had focused heavily on developing assessment for learning principles within English, Mathematics and Science, with little time available for focused whole school development in other subject areas.

Fortunately, this issue had also been highlighted by the school leadership team. As a result, a small number of additional subjects were selected as the next areas for focus for the development of assessment for learning. These subjects were chosen in collaboration with subject leaders and were selected based on a common need and desire to specifically develop the children's own involvement in the assessment of their skills in each subject area.

James was pleased that Geography had been selected as a focus subject for the development of assessment for learning and pupil self assessment. However, he also felt some trepidation because his experience of effective assessment in Geography was limited. Nevertheless, James knew that there were some very experienced colleagues with the school who were already confident in both their use of assessment for learning and teaching Geography. It was this knowledge that inspired James to create the Standards and Innovation Team (SIT).

It was proposed that the SIT would consist of a small group of colleagues, from different phases within the school, who were all equally confident about experimenting with assessment for learning in Geography. As James was unsure of the way in which the development of assessment for learning would progress, he chose to strategically use the SIT as a indicator of progress and next steps across the year (an example of James' actual subject development plan is provided on page 138). James had been concerned that his lack of confidence might lead him to implement experimental approaches to assessment at a whole school level that would ultimately prove unmanageable or inappropriate. In turn, this could lead his colleagues to suffer from 'initiative fatigue': they would quickly lose their momentum and commitment to assessment in Geography if they were repeatedly asked to fully embed an approach, only for it to be changed or completely discarded after a term or so.

Instead James chose to use the SIT to trial his approaches over a period of a few weeks. Having devised a potentially useful means of involving children in the assessment of their own subject skills, James would then ask the SIT of three staff to test the materials in their own classrooms. They were aware that they should not radically change their classroom practice in order to complete the trial, but simply test the approaches on a small group or individual pupils. James would then briefly meet with the SIT to discuss their progress and to take feedback on how his more experienced colleagues felt about his ideas.

This was professionally and personally very beneficial to James. In a professional sense, James was rapidly developing his own skills in assessment for learning, based on the practice of his colleagues. He could work through all the potential issues, amend less effective aspects and present evidence from actual classroom practice, *before* presenting his proposed model for assessment in Geography to the whole staff. On a personal level, James also found that he developed close working relationships with the colleagues in the SIT, some of whom he had only ever interacted with on a superficial level. As a result, James was able to draw upon these positive relationships to support him in future projects, and colleagues more readily approached James for support and advice in his areas of expertise.

Key Issue: Assessment in [subject] Priority: To develop approaches to assessment for learning in [subject]					
Impact on learning, progress and achievement Teachers will be able to more accurately assess their children in [subject], supporting their further development – as well as informing next steps and annual school reports to parents.					
Action				**Evaluation**	
Tasks	Staff leading	Timescale	Resources	Success criteria	Completed
• Subject leader to meet with Whole School Assessment Leader to review current assessment arrangements and links to skills based planning.	Subject leader	Term 1		• Subject leader has a clear understanding of current assessment practices and core principles of school policies.	
• Subject leader to review the quality of commercial assessment materials, assessing their suitability for our context.	Subject leader	Term 1		• Subject leader aware of the positive aspects of the commercial assessment materials, as well as those areas that we need to personalise to match the school context and pupils' needs.	
• Staff meeting to discuss the possible use of the commercial assessment materials, trialling this with the Standards and Innovation Team (SIT).	Subject leader	Term 2	Staff meeting	• All teaching staff are familiar with the materials and SIT can use them within subsequent [subject] sessions.	

• Subject leader to analyse assessment data produced by the (SIT) to moderate accuracy of assessments in comparison with samples of pupil work (pupil interviews combined to be conducted at the same time).	Subject leader	Terms 3 and 5	Staff meeting and half day release	• Subject leader clear about the accuracy of assessments made using the materials – identifying any aspects that need to be strengthened within the school.
• Subject leader to hold a staff meeting to share findings of SIT trial and to discuss the implementation of assessment materials with all staff.	Subject leader	Term 4	Staff meeting	• All staff aware of best practice in the use of materials from SIT trial and how to implement this in their own classrooms.
• Follow-up staff meeting to review the use of the commercial assessment materials, as a result of teacher trialling during Terms 3–5	Subject leader	Term 6	Staff meeting	• Subject leader and all staff agree final whole school approach to the use of the assessment materials.

Evaluation of impact

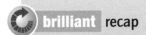 **recap**

The four most important messages from this chapter for the Brilliant Subject Leader are:

1   Your strategic subject development plan must be achievable. Be ambitious about the potential development of your subject but be realistic in your timescales.

2   It may take a little longer in the initial stages, but calculating potential time and financial requirements at the planning stage can make the task of fulfilling the plan much easier in practice.

3   If there is potential for collaboration with colleagues, use it to make better use of your time and that of your colleagues. You can be more ambitious (see point 1 above) if you have more hands available to complete the task!

4   Your subject development plan is *strategic* not *literal*. If necessary, adapt your planned actions and timescales whilst staying focused on the need to meet the original priority.

CHAPTER 8

Supporting and developing others

Throughout this book, we have repeatedly returned to our mantra of *work smarter, not harder* with the goal of placing this at the core of your role as a subject leader. Nowhere is this more important than when you consider the part you are expected to play within the continuing professional development (CPD) of your colleagues.

When accepting the mantle of subject leader for the first time, there is often considerable trepidation at the prospect of being perceived as the 'expert' in that curriculum area. This may be felt even more keenly when you factor in the significant part the subject leader plays in developing the subject knowledge, understanding and skills of the teachers and supportive staff in their team.

As has been emphasised in previous chapters, this pressure should not deter you from taking on the role. There are a number of practical, manageable and *smart* approaches to CPD that you can implement, which will avoid the need for you to spend many hours of *hard* labour toiling over textbooks, taking night classes or joining the Open University in order to become the world expert in British geology or the dietary requirements of natterjack toads!

this pressure should not deter you from taking on the role

Where do I start?

The potential avenues that could be followed within subject-based CPD are endless and it is possible for every subject leader to occupy all the available staff training sessions in a school, every year, twice over. However, it is clear that within a single school there will be a dozen or more subjects, and possibly an equivalent number of subject leaders, all requiring some opportunities to provide CPD for the staff in the school. The physical time and financial resources available for subject-based training is obviously finite and you, as a subject leader, therefore need to ensure that the CPD on offer for your subject is well focused and targeted precisely on specific and prioritised needs.

There are two important key questions to consider when you first begin to strategically plan any CPD opportunities. These are:

- What CPD is required for the staff in my team to be able to lead learning effectively for my subject area?
- What CPD do I require in order to support the needs of my colleagues?

As mentioned in the previous chapter, it is important to incorporate well focused CPD opportunities into the strategic development or action plan for your subject, to ensure that time and money are invested in those areas which will have the most impact on teaching, learning and curriculum standards. If you are going to devise an effective strategic plan, then you need to first answer these two key questions.

There are a number of different ways in which to access this information and the means by which you, as a subject leader, do so will depend greatly on the size and organisational structure of your school. Therefore, it may be helpful to summarise some of these approaches which you can select from and combine to meet the context of your own subject and school.

In order to establish the subject-specific CPD needs of the staff in your school you will most likely need to employ a mixture of formal and informal evaluation techniques. These might include:

- staff self-assessments;
- outcomes of lesson observations;
- feedback from individual line managers;
- external evaluations;
- externally imposed initiatives.

In isolation, each of the sources of evaluation will not necessarily provide you with an accurate picture of the CPD needs of your staff. However, if you make *smarter* choices about the elements that you choose to use within your own setting then you should be able to effectively and easily provide the right CPD for your staff and subject, without the need to work *harder* than you already are!

Staff self-assessments

If you are asking yourself, as a subject leader, what your staff need in order to more effectively lead learning in your subject area then you may, in the first instance, be asking the wrong person! All too often we can get caught up in the importance of our role as a subject leader, taking the weight of the educational world on our shoulders and applying an unreasonable expectation upon ourselves to be the font of all knowledge and to have some kind of innate ability to merely 'know' what your staff need by a process of osmosis. Go easy on yourself and ask the people you are trying to help – your colleagues!

ask the people you are trying to help – your colleagues

There are many different mechanisms to scaffold this important exchange of information and the process you choose will greatly depend on the individuals you are working with. In some cases, a staff questionnaire can provide an insight into the CPD needs of your team. The success of this approach relies greatly on the quality of the preparation of the questionnaire before it reaches the staff. In just the same way as we explored the manner in which questions need to be carefully formed for pupil interviews, the questions you ask your staff need to be selected with a clear purpose in mind.

It can be all too easy to fall into the trap of asking closed, procedural questions such as:

- Are you confident in teaching the subject?
- Do you have all the resources you need?
- Have you received any training in the last year?

The outcomes of such a questionnaire would certainly generate paperwork to be filed but, as you are hopefully now aware, merely filling folders and being busy with documents does not result in effective subject leadership. Instead you, as the subject leader, must be asking questions such as:

- What aspect of the 'subject' curriculum are you most confident in teaching?
- In which element/s of your teaching would you appreciate further support?
- Which areas of the 'subject' curriculum do your pupils find most challenging?

By asking these types of questions you will be moving beyond the 'box-ticking' exercise that can form the basis of many questionnaires, instead encouraging each staff member to reflect on their own practice and their own CPD needs.

In addition, the true success of this process lies in how you react to the information you have gained. Even with the most focused, professionally supportive questions, the self-assessment process will ultimately prove fruitless if the answers are simply read once and then filed away. The finished questionnaires should be considered as the seeds of CPD in your school which, with sufficient care and attention, can result in the strong and vibrant growth of the team.

brilliant tip

Don't be too ambitious with the number of questions you ask within any form on self-assessment for your staff. You are more likely to receive worthwhile and timely responses to your questionnaires if you have asked a smaller number of well-focused questions, as opposed to compiling an extensive 'interrogation' by paper. You may also find that asking closed or multiple-choice questions can be a false economy – the ease of responding in such a way might encourage a more rapid response from your staff, but the insight you gain may be limited by the nature of the responses themselves.

When you have collected all your questionnaires together (which in itself can be a challenge with a busy staff) then it is important that you review them individually but also as a cohort. In the first instance, you must look at the individual profiles of each staff member. What are their specific strengths and areas for development? Have they received sufficient CPD in recent times? Has this had a clear impact?

It can then be helpful to look across all the responses for trends. If a large number of your staff are struggling with a specific aspect of the curriculum, then that might be a priority area. However, remember that the questionnaires should act only as an indicator of the needs of your staff and that it is important to follow this up with your own evaluation. For example, difficulties being experienced by many staff in a specific aspect of the subject may be the result of poor resourcing or issues with curriculum structures (as addressed in Chapters 2 and 3) rather than a lack of professional knowledge, understanding and skills.

Finally, don't forget that subject leaders and teachers are also human beings! Very often it is the case that we will learn the most about our colleagues during everyday conversations and professional interactions. Therefore, use the outcomes of the questionnaire as a vehicle for discussion. Follow up on any responses that you don't fully understand, acknowledge any strengths that emerge and always give a simple 'thank you' for the time they have invested – this will help to nurture a positive attitude towards future CPD activities that you may lead or introduce.

> use the outcomes of the questionnaire as a vehicle for discussion

Outcomes of lesson observations

As discussed in previous chapters, lesson observations can provide subject leaders with a wealth of information in a relatively short space of time. Within a single hour-long lesson, you will be given an insight into pupil attitudes, the quality of curriculum resourcing, the implementation of curriculum planning and, most importantly for this chapter, the quality of teaching.

It is important to remember that the success of any leader relies greatly on the quality of those they lead. In your role as a subject leader, you cannot single-handedly provide high quality learning experiences in your subject, for all the pupils in the school. Neither can you assume that all your teachers can teach every aspect of the curriculum as effectively as possible. You must ensure that your teachers can provide those effective learning experiences in their own classrooms. As one of my own secondary school teachers stated, 'An army of 10,000 will not overcome an army of 10, if there are 10,000 wild monkeys and

10 trained men.' The key to success is effective leadership and development of the team.

Therefore, what you see in terms of teaching and learning in a classroom situation can help to highlight specific CPD needs for your colleagues, which you must then address and monitor closely. In these situations, the needs may be identified in different ways. In many cases, you will observe a lesson and become aware of certain aspects of the teacher's practice which could benefit from further training and support. When providing the feedback to your colleagues, you will often find that they too are aware of these needs and that the lesson observation has provided a useful opportunity for a focused discussion on how best to support the professional development of your colleague.

Equally, during a lesson observation you, as the observing subject leader, may identify specific areas of need which your colleague has yet to acknowledge for themselves. As discussed in Chapter 4, you will need to handle feedback carefully in these situations, supporting your colleague in acknowledging these needs themselves. This is an important step which can ultimately impact on the success of any future CPD. If you have a member of staff who feels that CPD is being unnecessarily imposed on them, without appreciating either the personal needs it is meant to address or the needs of the school, then the potential impact of any training and support can be diluted. However, if a colleague understands that any CPD provided is sharply focused on their own professional needs and is intended to improve the impact on the learning of the children in their classroom, then their interaction with the training opportunity will benefit from their own purposeful enthusiasm and desire to engage with the process as fully as possible.

In addition, the careful and considered communication of why CPD is necessary and beneficial can also impact on staff morale, as colleagues will feel valued and appreciated. This not only establishes a positive ethos around the way in which you, as a subject leader, make use of CPD within your subject area but will also enhance the teacher's performance in the classroom – happy teachers are usually effective teachers!

Feedback from individual line managers

In every school there should be clearly defined and professionally robust processes for the performance management of individual teachers within the school. Performance management can be an extremely useful mechanism for informing any programmes of CPD provided by the school. However, it is also important to acknowledge the confidential nature of performance management.

In the first instance, any performance management discussions between an individual member of staff and their line manager must remain confidential, being shared only with the headteacher (where the headteacher is not themself the line manager of the staff involved). Within these performance management discussions, targets are set to support the individual professional development of the member of staff, which also outline the expectations that the school has of that individual in terms of meeting the identified whole school priorities for development. However, should the member of staff agree with their line manager that they are happy for some of these priorities/ development needs to be shared with colleagues, who might be able to provide further support, then this can really empower a subject leader to have a significant impact on the development of their colleague.

The benefit of being party to CPD needs in relation to performance management stems from the professional and legal standing of the targets set within the process. When the performance management targets have been agreed, they form the basis of a professional agreement between the school leaders and the individual. This agreement requires the individual to perform in a sufficiently effective manner to meet the targets, with a commitment from the school to provide any and all reasonable forms of support in order for the individual to achieve these goals.

For you, as a subject leader, this means that any CPD that you are asked to provide in relation to performance management targets will receive an enhanced level of professional support and financial backing. Not only might this make your role as a coordinator/provider of CPD practically easier but it also helps to raise of the profile of your subject within the school.

We have already learnt that we do not have an automatic right to access any performance management information, other than our own. Nonetheless, it can be helpful to open a dialogue with the performance management line managers within your school. As more senior members of the staff, they should already be aware of the strategic plans you have in place for your subject and how these plans might influence the development of the staff in their line management teams, but it can also be useful to have a direct conversation with them,

> open a dialogue with the performance management line managers

highlighting your willingness to provide subject support and development for them or any members of their team. This approach also exemplifies that you are a proactive and supportive subject leader who is focused on maintaining and raising the quality of teaching and learning within your subject area.

External evaluations

In many local authorities, advisory teams are now more proactively supporting school self-evaluation by working alongside subject leaders to provide an objective view of the subject and its development within the school.

In the past, advisors may have visited schools only where there was a perceived 'issue' or a specific request had been made by the headteacher for the advisor to provide a particular programme of training and development. However, as part of an advisor's role is now to support schools in ensuring that their self-evaluation is effective, this provides subject leaders with an excellent opportunity to draw upon the expertise of a colleague from outside of their school context. In some cases this expert may be the advisor themselves or one of their team of leading teachers within the local authority.

Regardless of their role, simply having access to an individual who has had the benefit of observing practice in your subject in many different settings can really benefit you as a subject leader. They may well have seen some of the most, as well as possibly some of the least, effective practice in your local area. As a result, they should be able to provide you with some useful insights into new approaches to teaching and learning, identifying those which might most effectively benefit the colleagues in your school and the needs of your subject. An additional benefit of working closely with a colleague from the local authority is that they may have access to additional funding and resources which may support you in the delivery of any required CPD.

Another obvious source of external evaluations are national inspection teams such as OFSTED and SIAS (Statutory Inspections of Anglican Schools) inspectors. Whilst the physical process of an inspection can feel intense and pressurised, the preparation for these periodic inspections and the outcomes can prove useful. This will be explored in more detail in Chapter 11; however, it is worthwhile saying at this point that the evaluation schedules/frameworks provided by these bodies can help to direct your focus as a subject leader. Needless to say that, regardless of inspections and evaluations, our first priority is to ensure that the children in our schools are receiving the very best learning experiences possible. However, as a new subject leader, it can sometimes be challenging to siphon through all the available information and subject development needs in order to distil the most urgent areas for attention. This is also true for CPD. You might be aware that standards of teaching and learning aren't sufficiently high but you may be unsure exactly how to have a positive impact in these areas.

By referring to the extensive guidance provided by these professional bodies, it is possible to identify which aspects of classroom practice may need urgent support and development. As a result, you can then look more closely at the current provision within your own context and devise a programme of CPD to more effectively address the identified needs.

One caveat when making use of external sources of evaluation is to remember that, in any professional relationships with outside agencies, it is you and your colleagues who are in the best position to understand the particular context of your setting. External bodies can be useful at shining a light on those aspects of the school or subject which you have previously not been fully aware of, but how you address those needs must be meaningful and purposeful within the school context. As a leader of subject-specific CPD, you need to devise opportunities for training and support which match the needs and learning styles of your colleagues to ensure optimum impact and sustainable development.

Externally imposed initiatives

By its very nature, educational procedure and practice is under constant review as we strive to provide the best possible learning experiences for the children in our care. Inevitably, these reviews are often bound up with local and national politics. It is all too easy to become bogged down in the rights and wrongs of the political establishment and the impact this has upon

> educational procedure and practice is under constant review

education. Ultimately, as individual teachers and subject leaders we have very little influence over the political machinations of national bodies, advisory panels and thinktanks. However, what we *can* do is approach nationally imposed initiative and directives with the same professional rigour as we would with any other aspect of practice in our schools.

As mentioned earlier in this book, we must carefully filter the educational detritus of national initiatives from the sound educational theory and practice. When we have clarified what is most valuable for our own pupils and colleagues, we will then be able to evaluate the additional CPD that may be required in order to support our colleagues to effectively and efficiently develop their own classroom practice.

In the past, many subject leaders have understandably taken the extensive training manuals, resources and videos that have been provided at a national level, diligently delivering them to colleagues and taking confidence from the fact that the centrally prepared training materials had been comprehensively delivered to their colleagues in the school. However, there has long been a mismatch between the training materials associated with these national directives and the variety of school contexts nationally. It is a simple case of one size *not* fitting all!

On the other hand, I would not wish you to feel compelled to disregard any national or local training materials that arrive at your school; but you should always evaluate them fully before introducing them to your colleagues. So far, this chapter has focused on evaluating the CPD needs of your staff *before* implementing a training programme. The same rule should apply to national initiatives.

- Look closely at the materials; your school may actually have more effective practice already in place.

- What CPD materials are provided? Do they match your context? If not, don't use them as given, adapt them to make them meaningful to your setting and your staff.
- Is this CPD urgent? Just because it is a national directive does not necessarily put it above the identified priorities of the school. What is most important for the staff and children in your school?

In summary, when you are evaluating the CPD needs of your colleagues in relation to the development of your subject, it is essential that you follow the same principles as you would when evaluating the quality of teaching and learning across the school. In order to gain an accurate and worthwhile insight into the professional development needs of your colleagues, you must draw upon a variety of evidence from a variety of different sources. Some CPD needs will be immediately obvious, others will emerge only through further monitoring and evaluation. However, time and money are valuable and rare commodities in our schools; hence, it is vital that any programmes of CPD are meaningful, worthwhile and directly relate to the needs of colleagues.

At the start of this chapter, we asked two key questions:

- What CPD is required for the staff in my team to be able to lead learning effectively for my subject area?
- What CPD do I require in order to support the needs of my colleagues?

Hopefully, you now have a clearer picture of exactly how you can develop an accurate profile of the CPD needs within the team or school; but we must not forget your own needs.

I will reiterate that you do not need to be a degree-level archaeologist to lead History, a distant relation of Monet to lead Art or indeed an author to lead English! However, you may find that before you can effectively support colleagues in their professional development, you in fact need some further training and support yourself.

This training and development can be accessed in a number of different ways:

● your own professional reading/research;

● cluster training and collaboration;

● local authority training.

As with the various approaches to evaluating the CPD needs of your school, so there are also a variety of ways of meeting your own CPD needs. Initially, your CPD needs may have been identified by you and your line manager, independent of the needs emerging from the staff within your school. However, it is important to strike a balance between those areas you

there are a variety of ways of meeting your own CPD needs

need to develop in order to confidently lead the development of your subject and the skills you require in order to lead the development of your colleagues.

For example, a Science leader may find that they need to develop their understanding of aspects of the Science curriculum in order to ensure that the curriculum content within the school provides adequate coverage; whilst also requiring additional training in the teaching of investigative skills to allow them to lead a number of CPD sessions with the school staff. In this situation, the subject leader would need to refer back to their strategic development planning. Which of these areas (curriculum coverage/investigative skills) is the most urgent priority for the school? If they are both equally relevant, then additional funding might need to be sought from the headteacher to facilitate training in both these areas.

Essentially, you, as a subject leader, must think strategically. This will mean that, at times, you will need to prioritise staff training over your own, or vice versa. This decision can always be made easier by considering the overall impact on the learners in the school and which option will best serve their needs.

When you have achieved an appropriate balance in your training needs, you must then consider who will provide the CPD.

Your own professional reading/research

In recent years, the popularity of teachers conducting their own professional reading appears to have waned. Understandably, this seems to have coincided with the year-on-year increase in the workload of teachers and the constant challenge of trying to maintain a healthy work–life balance. With this in mind, it is important to note that when refer-ring to professional reading I am not suggesting that subject leaders arrive home after a busy day in the classroom, mark their books at home

> it is important to schedule professional reading

and then settle down for the few remaining minutes of the day to read the latest research report from the Department for Education! Instead, it is important to schedule professional reading as carefully as you would any other subject leader task.

For example, our desks can rapidly fill with mailings, local authority updates, research summaries and inspection find-ings over the space of a week. Whilst much of the paper that passes through our school will be filed in the recycling bin, it can be worthwhile to set aside 10–15 minutes to sift through these growing piles of documentation to, initially, dispose of any completely irrelevant information. This is where you need to be ruthless as a subject leader. When I say 'irrelevant', I mean anything that is not directly relevant to your CPD needs, those of the staff or the development of your subject as detailed in your strategic planning. We no longer have time to create folders of 'might be useful' information as, in practical terms, you will never actually get around to reading it: instead you are creating a pulsating folder of guilt which will nag away at your professional conscience every time you see it!

By ruthlessly editing this documentation, you will then be left with a small number of potentially powerful sources of information. This smaller number can be read through whilst waiting to start a lesson observation or during the vacant appointments at a parents' evening. The more weighty or complex reports or publications could be read at some other time, when at least you can be confident that you are committing your precious time to some professional reading that is ultimately going to benefit you and your school.

Obviously, as you are reading this book, you are clearly an individual who is committed to professional reading. Again, by clearly diagnosing your CPD needs as a subject leader you can make more effective use of the time you set aside for these activities so that you will be more focused on what it is that you are trying to achieve or develop. Equally, it can sometimes be helpful to discuss your professional reading with a colleague or line manager who is aiming to address similar professional goals. This may deepen your understanding of the reading you have completed, maximising its potential to have a positive impact on your own practice and that of others.

Cluster training and collaboration

In the current educational climate, many schools are aiming to achieve the same curricular goals, especially in the areas of curriculum structure and content. Therefore, all schools have a potentially rich source of CPD support available on their doorstep – the schools in their geographical or professional cluster.

It is now common practice for schools in the same cluster to synchronise some of their staff development and training days, in order to work collaboratively on shared CPD projects. For example, a renowned speaker might be invited to provide training to a number of schools within a cluster, for each of whom employing the speaker's services individually would not have been financially viable.

In the same vein, the concept of cluster collaboration and shared CPD is now filtering down to individual subject leaders. If schools open channels of communication at subject leader level, this dialogue often reveals that all the leaders of similar subjects are aiming to development or improve similar aspects of their subject. The combined efforts of two, three or more subject leaders on a common goal can make the journey much less arduous and ultimately beneficial to a more extensive number of learners.

This approach can also be applied to your own CPD: subject leaders can benefit from tapping into their local trade in knowledge! When you are trying to source a means of meeting your own CPD requirements, it is

> subject leaders can benefit from tapping into their local trade in knowledge

worth making contact with parallel colleagues in other schools as, chances are, there will be someone who has already received training in the aspect of subject leadership that you also require CPD. It is therefore possible for this colleague to cascade their training to you, on the understanding that at some point in the future, they might also be able to benefit from some of your expertise or experience in return. Accessing CPD in this way has a number of benefits:

- The CPD is contextualised: your colleague will have already applied the initial training to their own practical school context and may be able to share the pitfalls and how to avoid them!

- You are establishing a sustainable link that you may be able to call upon for purposes other than CPD. For example, you may initially share training materials between staff but this might eventually lead to groups of learners collaborating on shared projects, helping to enhance their curricular experiences.

● This form of CPD is cost effective. If meetings are arranged for out-of-school hours, you will not only save on conventional training costs but also the cost of supply teachers. This will then leave you with a CPD budget which can better support those CPD needs that can't be met through any other means than the use of an external provider.

Working with cluster colleagues is an excellent way of establishing a sustainable learning community, which will benefit staff, children and schools overall for many years.

Local authority training

An excellent source of CPD for teachers at all stages of their career can be found through local authority (LA) programmes. Obviously, as with any training programme, the local authority training can only be effective when:

● the objectives of the training session meet the needs of the subject leader;

● the training is followed up and implemented with a measurable impact when the subject leader returns to school.

One of the strengths of training provided by members of the LA advisory team is that they will have formulated the training course based on their broader knowledge and understanding of the subject area. For example, the leader of a LA training session may well be able to incorporate the latest subject developments that they have discovered through their contacts in other local authorities or national bodies. In addition to this, they should also be able to make reference to any existing good practice within your own LA (this links back to the previous discussion about collaborating with other local subject leaders).

The fact that LA training sessions usually take place at a shared training centre, away from your own school, can also be beneficial to you as a subject leader. As you are effectively 'removed' from your own setting during the training, with the subsequent benefits of being unable to take an urgent phone call, cover a class or talk to a parent who has dropped in, then you are also provided with the physical and mental space to reflect on your needs. You can leave the daily distractions at school for a short period (they will still be there when you get back!) and really focus on your own development as a subject leader and how you can have the most significant impact on the learners in your school. You also have the benefit of direct contact with members of the LA, which can be useful for on-going advice and support in the future.

The most significant factor in ensuring the effectiveness of the training received at a LA level is how the training is utilised when you have returned to school and all those distractions have returned again. It all too easy to take the collection of handouts, documents and helpful notes you have gathered during the training sessions and leave them in a pile on your desk for weeks, before discovering them again when their potency and impact may have been slightly diminished, through the simple passage of time. Instead you, as the subject leader, need to strategically consider how you will ensure that the LA training, which is often quite costly to the school and possibly your CPD budget, will have a significant and observable impact when you return to school.

One way in which to ensure this is to strategically timetable a follow-up training session within your school.

strategically timetable a follow-up training session

For example, the Design and Technology subject leader may have recently attended a training session focus on the use of and progression within pneumatics within learners' design projects. Such specialist training can easily be lost to the subject leader unless it is acted upon immediately. Therefore, within two weeks of the subject leader's training, they could deliver the same training to their colleagues with the result that the subject leader's learning has been cascaded to the rest of the team.

Alternatively, a subject leader may have attended a LA training session focused on effective planning and long-term curriculum structures in Modern Foreign Languages. If cascading this training would not appropriately meet the needs of the subject leader's colleagues, then they could instead schedule a period of subject leader release time in order to review and amend the long-term planning structures present in the school to incorporate the new elements from the training. The renewed planning could then be shared with colleagues at a later date and the changes implemented through subsequent long- and medium-term planning.

brilliant timesaver

When attending a LA training session, go armed with a memory stick or USB key. Rather than having to write copious notes during the training session and then devise your own training materials when you return to school, simply ask the trainer if you could download a copy of their presentation for your own use. On your return to school, all you need do is customise these materials to your own preferences and spend the time you would have committed to creating your own presentation preparing other supporting documents that your colleagues will find useful and supportive.

The difficulties that some schools experience when contemplating the use of LA trainers or sending staff to an external LA training course is the cost. You may well find that local authorities now provide a small number of 'free' or 'cashback' courses. These are usually targeted at subjects or aspects of education that the LA is trying to promote amongst all the schools in the area and, therefore, aim to encourage attendance through the removal of all apparent costs to the school. However, as a subject leader, you may also hold a CPD budget for your subject. It is important to remember that, whilst it may be free for you or one of your team to attend these training sessions, there may also be associated supply cover costs that must also be taken into consideration when releasing a member of staff.

There are obviously ways around this, such as running a system of flexible Planning, Preparation and Assessment (PPA), where subject leaders can choose to make use of their PPA time for training sessions which would help to save their allocated CPD budget, hence, enabling them to potentially access a higher number of external training courses. Clearly, senior or subject leaders cannot impose this on their staff, as all teachers are entitled to their 10 per cent (PPA) time. Alternatively, a senior member of staff who has no teaching commitment could be asked to cover class commitments of the staff member attending the training session.

brilliant example

Establishing a CPD network with other schools to develop subjects across the curriculum

Dominic had been subject leader for Maths for 18 months, following on from the completion of his NQT induction year. As he was still relatively new to the role and was keen for further CPD, he was invited to be the school representative within a non-geographical cluster group of schools.

The non-geographical cluster group had been set up by a group of like-minded headteachers who wished to explore the potential for schools to collaborate on the self-evaluation of their curriculum and the validation of the judgements made during the self-evaluation process.

Dominic attended the initial cluster meeting with colleagues from the other schools in the group to discuss the principles of the meta-evaluation project, to be called the ESSE group (Evaluating School Self-Evaluation). The initial meeting was also used for each subject leader to share their own CPD needs and that of their staff, in order for a shared focus to be agreed to facilitate the project and to encourage collaboration.

Following discussions with colleagues from other schools, Dominic established a common focus of problem solving in Maths with two other schools. Each school had quite different contexts but each shared the desire to develop the way in which problem solving skills were taught to their learners, at all stages of the primary school.

It was then agreed that each group of three schools, the Evaluation Triads, would work together over a number of weeks to devise an evaluation schedule. Dominic had recently attended a training session on the use of the new OFSTED framework and how this applied to the role of the Maths subject leader. As a result, he took the lead in supporting his colleagues to devise a series of key quality indicators which could be used to moderate the self-evaluation of Maths in each of the three schools.

When the evaluation schedule had been completed, each of the subject leaders in Dominic's Evaluation Triad agreed to conduct their own self-evaluation of problem solving in Maths for their school using the agreed criteria. The evaluation schedule that Dominic and his colleagues had devised also required the subject leader to provide the evidence for their judgements.

Dominic volunteered to be the first to complete the evaluation schedule, due to his recent OFSTED training. He also felt that his school required the most significant development in terms of their approach to the teaching of problem-solving skills. The self-evaluation process took Dominic one afternoon, the release time for which was provided by his headteacher. During the process, Dominic drew together all his subject leader monitoring and evaluation from the start of the year to the present, extracting any elements which related directly to problem-solving skills teaching. Dominic also chose to 'grade' the quality of teaching and learning for problem solving skills, using an adapted version of the OFSTED criteria which had been built into the ESSE evaluation schedule.

Upon completion of the self-evaluation, Dominic then emailed the documents to his Evaluation Triad colleagues in the partner schools. At this stage the two partner schools met, without Dominic present, to review his self-evaluation and to devise some questions that would help to validate Dominic's self-evaluation (such as seeking further clarification of standards) and they also identified aspects that they felt could lead to improvements in the quality of teaching and learning of problem solving skills in Dominic's school. Their feedback was then emailed back to Dominic in preparation for his colleagues' visit to his school.

The purpose of the visit to his school was to allow Dominic to present his evidenced responses to the questions that had been raised and to also collaboratively explore the potential for future development. Dominic and his colleagues felt that this element of the project was an important means by which they could prepare themselves for future OFSTED inspections in a supportive way. If they could respond to the questions from their critical friends in the Evaluation Triads, then they would be in a better position when faced with the prospect of an interview with an OFSTED inspection.

During the visit, Dominic presented his evidenced responses to his colleagues' questions, resulting in them validating his judgements. This was instrumental in confirming for Dominic that he had a firm grasp on the development of Maths, from the perspective of the subject leader, as up to this point he had received very little feedback on the way in which he was performing in his leadership role. The remainder of the day was focused on how the teaching of problem-solving skills could be improved in Dominic's school. This was a really valuable process for Dominic, as all the members of the Evaluation Triad were focused on a single school – Dominic's – and they were combining their experience to benefit the children in the school. By the end of the visit, they had developed a progression of skills for the teaching of problem solving and had made adaptations to the weekly ▶

Maths planning format to encourage teachers to incorporate some explicit problem-solving skills teaching into every session. Dominic found the experience both empowering and motivating.

The same process was completed for the two other schools in the Evaluation Triad. In each case, the subject leaders felt invigorated by the experience and motivated to forge forward with the development of problem solving within their schools.

Whilst the project definitely had a short-term impact in each of the three schools, in the area of problem solving, Dominic also discovered longer-term benefits. Over the extended period that the schools had worked together on the ESSE project, they had learnt a great deal about each of the schools with their knowledge extending beyond simply that of the Maths curriculum. Over the subsequent months, Dominic was instrumental in establishing additional links between subject leaders in his own school and those in the other triad schools. As a result, many of these subject leaders also adopted the ESSE project framework, in order to facilitate the development of their own subject areas.

 **brilliant** recap

The four most important messages from this chapter for the Brilliant Subject Leader are:

1   Be clear about the CPD needs of your staff, before attempting to provide any training.

2   Strategically plan your own CPD, as a subject leader, as well as that of your colleagues.

3   Consider which is the most appropriate means of providing CPD for you and your staff: in-house training, cluster training or an external provider.

4   However CPD is provided, ensure that there is a clear and measurable impact on standards of teaching and learning as a result.

CHAPTER 9

ICT across the curriculum

The ability to view any global location in seconds; communicating in hundreds of different languages; instant understanding of what is happening around the world at any given time; the capacity to answer virtually any question. Sound like the profile of a superhero or international spy? Well, in actual fact, this could be the profile of any child sitting in our classrooms on a daily basis. The advent of applications such as Google Earth, Twitter, Wikipedia and a whole range of Web 2.0 technologies that are constantly evolving have opened up a whole new world to the children of today. The use of ICT has now become integrated into the daily lives of many of our pupils and this integration is set to continue for the foreseeable future.

As educators and school leaders, we can take one of two routes: bury our heads in the sand and tell ourselves that we can teach in just the same way as we always have; or take on the exciting challenge of evaluating new technologies and developing our teaching to provide relevant and motivational learning experiences for the children in our schools. As a subject leader, you are in a powerful and influential position. You can spearhead the development of your subject curriculum to ensure that relevant and empowering forms of technology are embraced by your colleagues, leading to potentially better and more contextualised outcomes for the pupils.

> ensure that relevant and empowering forms of technology are embraced

In this role, it is essential that you proactively and professionally evaluate the potential impact of ICT in your subject area and take steps to ensure that the curriculum on offer is relevant and structures learning in the most effective way, including the use of ICT.

Historically, the step forward from chalk to pen led to a revolution in the teaching of penmanship to the masses; the introduction of heating and food into our schools prior to compulsory education meant that many reluctant children stayed at their desks and the advent of the BBC Personal Computer seeded the current use of computer technology in our schools today. It was over 25 years ago that the cream and brown casings of the now legendary BBC computers first landed in many of our schools. I personally recall many fond hours playing 'Granny's garden' on a BBC computer in my own primary school classroom, whilst my teacher kept a respectful distance and allowed us to discover what mysteries lay beyond the blocky graphics and pixelated text.

To future generations, these computers and their simplistic programmes will be the technological equivalent of cave paintings – however, from these humble beginnings we now find ourselves working in schools which live and breathe through technology. Computer technology, in many different shapes and sizes, is now so thoroughly embedded in all aspects of teaching and learning that schools are becoming educational cyborgs: biological and technological assets working in harmony towards a common goal. As educationalists and subject leaders, we must ensure that the potential of this technology is appropriately harnessed, skilfully managed and utilised in a meaningful manner which benefits the education of the children in our schools. If this is successfully achieved, the use of ICT in all aspects of your role is a key component in ensuring that you are indeed *working smarter, not harder*!

In your role as a subject leader, you need to ask yourself two key questions in order to ensure that ICT is being used effectively to support teaching and learning in your subject area. These are:

- How is ICT currently being used to support teaching and learning?
- How could I make this use of ICT more effective?

However, before we are able to explore these questions in detail, it is essential that we develop a shared understanding of *why* ICT is relevant to teaching and learning across the curriculum. As a subject leader, you too may need to develop this kind of shared understanding with your colleagues; sadly, there are still some individuals within the profession who fail to appreciate the educational potential inherent within modern technology. Leading by example can be a good approach

> leading by example can be a good approach

with these individuals and developing a degree of 'contagious enthusiasm' can be helpful – share positive experiences regularly and incidentally to show that ICT is part of everyday school life, not a bolt-on.

Why is it important to consider the use of technology across the curriculum?

Technology has become more and more prevalent in our daily lives. Many of us interact with some form of ICT on a daily, if not an hourly basis. Reading the news online; managing our banking electronically through our phones; listening to MP3 music tracks during gym sessions; and avoiding the traffic black-spots on our weekend breaks using the car's built-in GPS. The list is endless with new forms and uses of technology emerging on a virtually daily basis.

In recent history, this technological revolution has led to the coining of terms such as 'digital literacy' and 'digital communication'. The apparent trend has been to take an existing skill set that we have conventionally taught in schools and merely to add 'digital' as a prefix. This has done little to support the effective integration of ICT into our schools, as the development of the skills, knowledge and understanding necessary for our children to make efficient use of technology to support their own learning has been viewed as a 'bolt-on' to the existing curriculum structure. So too has the use of the same technology, across the curriculum, been seen as an optional extra.

In fact, terms such as 'digital literacy' are complete misnomers. We must be clear that, for example, literacy and English language skills are the same regardless of the media being used to record, share or express our thoughts. Whether a child is communicating their learning through a hand-drawn poster, a written essay, a blog or a video clip is irrelevant; it is the subject-specific learning and skills development that can be found at the core of the activity which is important. What is ultimately of the greatest relevance is which of these differing vehicles for communication is best suited to the needs of the individual learner, in order to most effectively support them in expressing their own ideas and opinions. At a medium-term or short-term planning stage, don't forget that your colleagues should be considering the incorporation of ICT alongside the learning objective in the same 'automatic' manner as they would for differentiation within a lesson or selecting the best resources to use.

It is also true that, just as English and Maths have long been considered essential life skills and key components in preparing children for productive and rewarding experiences in the world of work, ICT has also become an essential tool in many work places. Therefore, it is crucial that the children in our schools are fully prepared for their adult lives and the multimodal workplace experiences ahead of them. As teachers and subject leaders, we have no choice but to ensure that we are making the most effective use of ICT in our schools, in order to provide relevant and meaningful learning experiences for our pupils.

That's the ICT subject leader's job ... isn't it?

Another important distinction to make, before moving on to the development of ICT in your subject, is the unique role of the subject leader. In much the same way as the use of ICT in education has been misunderstood by an ever-decreasing number of colleagues, so too has there been a misinterpretation of the role of the subject leader.

It is true that prior to the birth of early computers in schools, the role of the ICT subject leader didn't exist and wasn't needed. Instead, schools would have had a caretaker or member of staff who was a bit

> the role of the subject leader has rapidly developed over the past 10 to 20 years

handy with a cassette recorder or knew their way around the new Polaroid camera. The role of the subject leader has rapidly developed over the past 10 to 20 years; however, the understanding of their role by colleagues has not moved at the same pace.

Let me pose some simple questions – is the English subject leader responsible for every piece of writing that takes place in the school, regardless of subject or purpose? Should the Maths subject leader monitor every calculation performed, graph drawn or table devised? To respond with anything but '*no*' to both these questions would be preposterous. Why then do many schools view the use of *all* technology in schools, regardless of subject or context, to be the responsibility of the ICT subject leader?

It is time to readdress this balance and you, as a subject leader, can make a substantial contribution to this. The relationship between the ICT subject leader, leaders of other subject areas and the use of technology across the school can be clarified in three points:

1   The ICT subject leader is responsible for the use of technology within the school to support the *teaching and learning of specific skills within the ICT curriculum.*

2 All subject leaders must take responsibility for ensuring that *ICT is used effectively to support teaching and learning in their subject area.*

3 The ICT subject leader and leaders of other subjects should work *collaboratively* to ensure that ICT skills are being developed in *meaningful contexts across the curriculum.*

The most important element of this relationship is collaboration. An effective subject leader will understand the potential impact of ICT on the teaching and learning in their subject, seeking support from the ICT subject leader to ensure that this is as effective as possible. An effective ICT subject leader will ensure that new technologies and current uses of ICT are proactively shared with other colleagues, leading to their use across the curriculum. Do you know who the ICT subject leader is in your school? Take care not to be confused by the role of ICT technician in your school, as the two roles are often distinct. To put it simply, the technician fixes ICT and the ICT subject leader guides the use of the technology. Why not spend some time getting to know both people, as there will definitely be times when you need guidance on the use of ICT – and certainly periods where you need the technology fixed quickly!

How is ICT currently being used to support teaching and learning?

Having established the vital nature of a partnership between the ICT subject leader and those leaders of other subjects within the curriculum, we can now explore the first of our two key questions in this chapter: 'How is ICT currently being used to support teaching and learning?'

The amount of technology available in schools will vary greatly depending on available funding, the priorities in the school and the geography of the school building itself. However, in many schools, the most prevalent form of technology in the classroom has changed from the large, stand-alone PC of yesteryear, with the focus now shifting to interactive whiteboards.

> which items of ICT equipment are actually in use?

Take a walk around your school – what technology is most obvious and, more interestingly, which items of ICT equipment are actually in use?

For many subject leaders and teachers, trying to assess the use of the whole range of technology on offer in a school in one fell swoop could be deemed over-ambitious and overwhelming. Instead, focusing on the use of interactive whiteboards can be a good starting point when reviewing the provision of ICT in a particular subject. The reason for this is that interactive whiteboards are very obvious (even the most technophobic teachers find them hard to ignore), they can be used by both teacher and children, and they are versatile.

As a subject leader, you need to establish whether these powerful tools are being used to their full potential. For example, there is a difference between using an interactive whiteboard as a mere (very expensive) form of display in a lesson, as opposed to using it to encourage the pupils to share their ideas or to stimulate discussion and creative thought.

In terms of developing your understanding of how ICT is used across your subject area, then the tools you need are the same as those we have discussed in our chapters on auditing provision and monitoring the standards in your subject. A lesson observation is an excellent means of establishing how effectively ICT is being incorporated into teaching and learning on a daily basis, as it provides you with a snapshot of what is hopefully regular and consistent practice. However, it is important to remember that this evidence must be used in combination with other forms of monitoring and evaluation to provide you with a fully rounded picture of the ICT provision in your subject area.

For example, a single lesson observation might suggest that ICT is thoroughly embedded within the teacher's daily practice, but when you examine weekly and medium-term planning there may be little or no reference to the use of ICT across this longer period. Has the teacher simply put together an 'all singing, all dancing' lesson using ICT for the purpose of the lesson observation? Are they using ICT regularly but not reflecting this in the planning? Is the teacher sufficiently confident with ICT? Do they understand the potential applications of ICT in supporting the teaching and learning within their subject? As you can see, the need to gather sufficient evidence in order to triangulate your understanding of the current ICT provision in your subject is crucial to your successful leadership of this area. By doing so, not only do you gain another insight into an important aspect of your subject but you are also empowered to have a greater potential impact on the learning experiences of the pupils in your school.

 **brilliant** timesaver

You need to know how ICT is being used in your subject area. Chances are that the ICT subject leader will also be monitoring how ICT skills are being taught across the curriculum. This provides an excellent opportunity for some timesaving collaboration! In addition to drawing on your own monitoring and evaluation of the subject as a source of evidence for ICT use, why not speak to the ICT subject leader to make use of their experiences? They may well have observed a lesson, in your subject area, where they were focused on how the ICT curriculum was being addressed in context. For example, they may have observed a Design and Technology lesson where ICT was being used to support children in producing a design schematic. This would provide the ICT subject leader with evidence of skills teaching in the modelling strand of ICT, whilst also giving you as the DT subject leader further exemplification of how ICT is being used to support teaching and learning in your subject. Extra evidence for your investigations, without having to commit the extra hour to observe the lesson in person: *working smarter, not harder*!

We have already discussed that starting with a review of the way in which interactive whiteboards are used in your school to support teaching and learning in your subject can be a comfortable and familiar point of entry for both you and your staff. In addition, there are also other areas of your subject and the way in which ICT is used that it may be useful to review. These might include the use of ICT for:

- **Communication**: Are children able to use technology to communicate their understanding in a variety of ways, moving beyond pen and paper to use video, blogging, wikis and email to reach a broader audience?

- **Interpretation**: Is ICT being used to support pupils in understanding complex or abstract ideas, such as analysing a Shakespearian text or tracking demographic changes over the last 100 years?

- **Stimulation**: Are your colleagues making the best use of ICT to capture the imaginations of their pupils through listening to topical discussions through podcasts, watching streaming video of breaking news, videoconferencing with the international space station or viewing a time-lapse video of insect metamorphosis?

- **Consolidation**: Can teachers more effectively recap on learning and recapture salient teaching points, such as revisiting pupils' questions recorded using MP3 or video files at the start of a project to evaluate how much learning has taken place; or using an online model to reinforce the life cycle of a flowering plant after growing real examples over the term?

- **Cohesion**: Is technology being used to merge learning at home and school, allowing parents to gain a clearer insight into the kinds of learning taking place in the classroom, or allowing a child to seamlessly transfer their learning activities between home and school using a learning platform?

How are others using ICT in my subject area?

Another important area in terms of ICT provision in your subject, which can often be overlooked, is the use of technology by support staff to aid pupils with their learning. Many schools and subject leaders rightly invest considerable resources into training their teaching staff to confidently make use of technology to support teaching and learning, yet the training needs of support staff are sometimes ignored. There is a considerable degree of wasted potential here, has ICT has the innate ability to motivate and aid pupils with special needs. Those pupils invariably spend much of their time with teaching assistants and other support staff, who may not necessarily have the ICT competence or confidence to maximise on those precious learning opportunities. (An example of how ICT training was provided to a group of English specialist support staff is detailed in the case study at the end of this chapter.) It is therefore important to spend some time evaluating the use of various technologies by support staff, establishing any pockets of good practice and seeking out opportunities for further development. Some possible areas could include:

- the use of MP3 recorders with dyslexic children to record initial ideas;
- incorporating mind-mapping software for children with sequencing needs;

- using video to record portions of lessons for later review with adult support or at home;

- using games and short, focused online activities to reinforce taught skills;

- using voice recognition software to support those with physical or mental learning needs.

As a subject leader, you should be seeking opportunities to promote the use of ICT in your subject by teaching assistants as this is a way in which you can initiate a groundswell of embedded ICT use. In much the same way as my earlier point about the term 'digital literacy' being irrelevant as digital technologies should be internalised within 'literacy' rather than considered as external 'bolt-ons'; the use of ICT within the classroom needs to be matter of fact and integral. When your pupils, teachers and support staff are making use of some technology on a daily basis, as part

> ICT within the classroom needs to be matter of fact and integral

of their normal practice, then you are in a strong position as a subject leader to take the development of subject-linked ICT to the next level. You will already have a team of willing individuals behind you, helping you to *work smarter, not harder*, as they will understand and appreciate the power of ICT as a learning tool; leading to them being open to the new developments that you might implement.

What ICT resources are available for my subject?

This is where you will benefit from the support of the ICT subject leader at your school. In most schools there is a plethora of different ICT hardware and software which only the ICT subject leader or school technician is fully aware of and can use. It is therefore worthwhile spending some time with one of the individuals, in order to explore the current resources and how they might be used.

However, as we have already mentioned, the ICT subject leader cannot be expected to know *your* subject area inside out, so some preparation will be needed on your part. You will need to spend some time considering which aspects of your subject curriculum might already lend themselves to being enhanced and supported through ICT. For example, the English subject leader might wish to explore aspects of drama/speaking and listening which could be developed; or the RE subject leader might be interested in how ICT could help to deepen children's understanding of particular religious ceremonies and rituals.

Starting the conversation with your ICT subject leader colleague with a question such as: 'What resources do we have to support storytelling?' or 'Do we have any software to help the teachers to cover data handling in Maths?' will help to set the tone for a professional dialogue where you are both making a valuable contribution and which is focused on enhancing the learning experiences for children and supporting teachers in effectively structuring their lessons.

brilliant tip

If you are trying to explore the potential uses of ICT within your subject, but your own ICT knowledge needs development, a good place to start can be your local authority scheme of work for ICT or a commercially published ICT scheme of work. Due to the need for the development of children's ICT skills to be contextualised, many schemes of work will have already made some links between their detailed ICT skills teaching and other areas of the curriculum. This will often come in the form of a few bullet-pointed exemplars within a planned unit of work, or a reference table linking particular ICT skills to other areas of the curriculum. These can act as excellent starting points to fire your own creativity. They will also occasionally reference particular pieces of hardware and software that might help.

Another aspect of the ICT provision for your subject to explore with the ICT subject leader, especially if you are new to the role, is the use of any subscription-based software services. Increasingly, software companies are now making their products available through online services or cached content (a regularly updated library of resources is downloaded to a specialised server in your school). Common resources found in schools include Espresso, GridClub, EducationCity and Clipbank. This is an excellent way of accessing current and relevant teaching resources to support your subject areas, and often provides teachers and pupils with the versatility of being able to access the content from any computer with an internet connection, during or beyond the school day. However, as a potential subject budget holder, you also need to be aware of how this is funded. Does the school's ICT budget cover the annual subscription cost? If it is a cross-curricular resource, is it part funded from your subject budget? Is the service being used effectively by staff and is its use sustainable?

> you also need to be aware of how this is funded

The final question is of greatest relevance. As we have discussed in previous chapters, you will be expected to provide value for money when purchasing equipment and resources. If you are spending what may be a substantial amount of your budget on an online, subscription-based service, then you need to assess whether it is being used effectively by your colleagues. Equally, you will need to consider the ongoing costs associated with this service before promoting its use amongst your staff. It wouldn't be an effective use of time or money if you encourage staff to embed a subscription service into their weekly and medium-term planning, for the service to be lost after 6 or 12 months as a result of budget constraints.

There are two simple ways of assessing the value and use of a subscription-based service already in use at the school:

- **Ask the pupils**: If they know what the resource is and can talk about it in detail, then chances are that it is at least being used regularly. You can then spend time investigating how effectively it is being used.

- **Ask the provider**: As the services are often hosted online, school users will be issued a password. As a marketing and tracking tool, many providers will monitor the frequency of user log-ins and in some cases will be able to provide profiles of how the product was used. For example, they might be able to issue you with a usage summary which tells you that a selection of year groups have been using the whole service extensively and regularly, whilst another year group have been using the resources more discretely at key points across the year. You could then use this information to more effectively target expenditure in the future.

Ultimately, it is essential that you have a solid understanding of the ICT resources available for your subject, regardless of format, which are *already present* in your school. All too often, successive subject leaders make purchases of resources and software which then, through simple lack of awareness on the part of colleagues, sit in cupboards and on computer networks collecting real or virtual dust! If you can establish what is available, and maybe even reintroduce your staff to some forgotten gems, then you can quickly and economically have a positive impact on the provision for ICT in your subject area.

How could I make the use of ICT more effective?

Having established exactly what the current status of subject-specific ICT is in your school, what resources are presently available and how effectively they are being used, it is possible to look for ways of enhancing that provision with the goal of ensuring that teaching and learning in your subject is as effective as possible.

The areas for development and possibilities for enhancement will vary greatly from school to school and across subjects. However, in this section we will explore how you can collaborate with colleagues to plan and implement curriculum enhancements, involving ICT, as well as considering some significant ICT developments and how they might impact on your school and your subject.

As mentioned previously, any development involving ICT is going to be benefitted by the fostering of a groundswell of positive support for the use of technology to support teaching and learning in your subject. For many colleagues, their own use of ICT is an area of perceived weakness or trepidation, so the prospect of being required to present these self-imposed inadequacies before a group of 30 very techo-confident children can be completely terrifying. Therefore, developments in ICT need to be implemented with an approach which encourages colleagues to feel part of the development process, rather than the development being 'done to them', within which they either succeed or fail.

The best way to achieve this is through practical exemplification. For many colleagues, the lack of engagement with ICT is the result of a lack of understanding. If a teacher doesn't understand the concept of a blog, then why would they even attempt to incorporate it into their teaching? Alternatively, as a subject leader, your demonstration of the use of a blog with a group of pupils or sharing examples from other schools might then encourage your colleague to experiment with the technology. Their subsequent attempt to use a blog for collaborative writing amongst a small group of pupils will then start them on a journey towards more extensive and complex uses of ICT, which you can support them with, as they build on prior successes.

> encourage your colleague to experiment with the technology

Building on prior successes and contextualised application is essential within any subject-based ICT development. We, as teachers, are too busy to be wasting time on projects which have no direct, positive impact on our classroom practice and cannot sustain repeated 'failures' within new approaches to teaching which impact on the learning in our classrooms. This is certainly true with ICT. If a teacher tries to make use of new software and hardware once and fails, then the chances of them trying to do so again are significantly reduced.

However, if you support them in trying something new, on a small scale, in their own classroom, providing assistance to troubleshoot the inevitable technical difficulties, you help to lay the foundations for future experimentation and development. The assistance does not necessarily need to come directly from you. It can be just as effective for you to work with a year group team or colleagues with similar needs, in order to plan and 'test-run' a lesson activity, which the colleagues then support each other to conduct within a classroom setting. Equally, using your role as subject leader to allow you to team-teach with a colleague can provide the supportive atmosphere needed for teachers to more confidently utilise technology in their daily teaching.

The methodology will vary according to your setting; however, the principle of contextualising the use of ICT and ensuring success, no matter how small, is an effective approach to promoting technology in your subject area.

Some common areas where subject leaders have identified areas for development in the use of ICT to support teaching and learning are explored below.

Support differentiation within a subject area

Commonly, reluctant learners or those who suffer from low self-confidence or self-esteem in a subject area are motivated by the use of ICT. Obviously, it is essential that the learning objective for these pupils has parity with their peers in the classroom, but by adapting the approach to incorporate an online content creator, such as Scratch or Twine, the pupils may be drawn into the learning activity with greater ease. Equally, for higher ability pupils, ICT can offer a wider audience and a broader context for pupils to apply their learning to; extending their class-based learning to consider the implications in the real world or to gain access to others' opinions of their learning, such as the use of a blog to share writing and ideas with others and to initiate a discussion.

Enhance the teaching of investigative skills in Science

A simple digital camera or video recorder can have a powerful impact in a Science lesson; simply record the pupils' questions and observations prior to an investigation. When it comes to concluding the investigation, the recordings can then be played back and the pupils can reflect on their learning in a more dynamic and motivating manner. This is also a good way of capturing and sharing ideas across the class; especially for those who might not openly address the whole class of their own volition. In addition, I would challenge anyone not to be enthralled by the hidden worlds revealed through a digital microscope – a world which can be shared through an interactive whiteboard rather than being an isolated experience for the single person looking through the lenses.

Develop evaluative skills in PE, particularly gymnastics

Digital audio and visual technology is now considerably more affordable. As such, many schools are now investing in commercially available and conventionally familiar technology within an educational context. For example, the use of Flip Video recorders in PE sessions can be a powerful tool. Multiple handsets can be bought for a few hundred pounds, allowing pupils to independently record gymnastic routines or sporting techniques and, in a matter of seconds, view the outcomes on screen or load this directly onto a computer to be shared with others. The individual being recorded can then observe for themselves where their technique could be improved, in combination with feedback from their peers.

Provide a meaningful purpose for speaking and listening activities

Many children are motivated by performing. Part of this motivation stems from the feedback received from the audience. Traditionally, the audience for any performance would be the peer group in the classroom, unless it is a heavily organised school production with parents invited to attend. Using video technology and online services such as YouTube or podcasting applications can provide an immediate audience from many different backgrounds. It might also spark links with other educational settings that can be built on in the future.

> many children are motivated by performing

Contribute to the development of data handling and interpretation skills in Maths

Whilst there is a place for drawing graphs and 'number crunching' within our curriculum, if you are trying to develop pupils' interpretative skills in Maths, then these activities can often get in the way. There is now a range of software available, in conjunction with web-based services such as Gapminder, which will provide pupils with data on a range of topics, which they can then analyse and interpret. The data sets can be customised and amended to meet the needs of the learners within the session, but removes the hurdle of having to create the chart or graph before you can examine what it shows.

Support the development of artistic skills and techniques using digital media

There is now an endless array of image manipulation software available, both free and commercial, which can be used to enhance, not replace, artistic activities in the classroom. Many pupils will have access to software such as Photoshop at home and may regularly use this technology to adapt their own digital images. Why not incorporate this into the curriculum? It is possible to take a digital image and manipulate colours, tones, lighting and perspectives to create an adapted or entirely new image. For those pupils who tentatively approach art, the added confidence provided by the 'undo' button in a software package can encourage them to experiment more freely and potentially achieve more as a result of their increased confidence.

How can I lead the developments when I'm not ICT confident?

As we discussed in the previous chapter, the mantle of subject leader does not automatically grant you with a mystical ability to know everything about the school curriculum! There may well be aspects of your subject and the associated use of ICT for which you will personally require support and development in order to lead across the school. Do not be afraid to seek this support; and it is essential that you do so before attempting to lead your colleagues. ICT is one of those areas of the curriculum that it is not easy to bluff your way through! Indeed, many of us have found our feet with new software by 'playing around' with it for a while, or observing others. This approach is fine for our own personal use of ICT; however, when leading others in their use of subject-specific ICT, this approach can lead to wasted time and effort. When you have scheduled a staff meeting or have been allocated a time within a staff development day to introduce a new ICT development within your subject, your colleagues will inevitably look to you as the expert – even if you are not! In these situations, you cannot afford to stumble your way through the demonstration of the technology, as you may well lose the commitment of your colleagues and their willingness to 'have-a-go' may wane.

allocate some time for your own development

Instead, allocate some time for your own development. This might be formally arranged, as mentioned in the previous chapter, or incidentally scheduled throughout the year. In terms of ICT, there are a number of different sources that you could call upon in order to enhance your skills and to support you in leading the next ICT development within your subject. Some of these sources of support might include:

- The ICT subject leader.
- The school technician.
- A colleague in your team who already displays confidence and good practice in your target area.
- A colleague from another school who has already implemented the same or a similar development.
- A software company representative or trainer: many such individuals will give you their time freely – you might just have to commit a little more time to listen to their sales pitch!
- In some cases, the children might help. If they are proficient in the use of the technology that you plan to present to colleagues, then let them teach you. It will help to support you, whilst also giving them a rewarding and contextualised learning experience.

It can also be helpful to look at the use of ICT beyond the walls of your school. There will undoubtedly be some form of ICT conference, cluster meeting or showcase in your local authority or region. These are not 'ICT leader clubs'; they are in most cases open to any interested parties from education. Why not attend one of these meetings or conferences – you will be surrounded by the examples of the best ICT practice which will be contextualised. You also have the added benefit of being able to speak to colleagues who have already experimented with technology, so you can learn how to avoid the pitfalls and how to maximise the impact on the learning in the classroom.

What national initiatives might I need to consider as a subject leader?

Whilst technology and educational ICT is constantly undergoing development and change, there are some current priorities worthy of consideration, as they have broad-ranging implications for schools in general and teachers in their subject leadership roles.

● **Learning platforms and Virtual Learning Environments**: Nationally all Local Authorities have been exploring different approaches to the implementation of personalised, online learning spaces for all learners. In some cases, schools have chosen their own commercial providers, whereas other schools have followed the LA-endorsed provider. The consideration needed from subject leaders is how best to use these online learning spaces to benefit the pupils in their schools. For example, a subject leader might wish to establish an online learning space with information and guidance for parents who wish to further support their child at home. Alternatively, a subject leader might choose to use their online learning space to structure homework, with pupils downloading learning tasks and uploading their response. There are a myriad of potential uses, but each subject leader and school needs to devise an appropriate strategic plan in order to remain in pace with the changing technological landscape at a national level.

● **Mobile computer technology**: Handheld computer
  devices are now common place in the home, in the form
  of mobile phones, smart-phones and tablet PCs. However,
  many schools are yet to utilise such technology within their
  own settings when, in fact, the hardware will already be
  sitting in many pupils' school bags. Subject leaders should
  start to consider how the lesson content for their subjects
  could be delivered more readily over wireless networks and
  across the internet, in formats that can be read by these
  mobile devices. If pupils spend a high percentage of their
  time interacting with these devices, then does it not make
  sense for course content, learning materials or stimulus
  tasks to be made available to our children in this way?

These are just two of the areas that are currently on the national
agenda. There will be others and priorities will change. The most
important consideration when exploring any form of technology
within your subject area is ensuring that there is a meaningful
purpose. There are many aspects of ICT which are 'gimmicky',
providing great fun but little educational value. The gimmicks
have their place as a recreational
tool but we cannot afford to waste
time on such aspects of ICT in our
already busy curriculum timetables.
Always approach the use of ICT objectively, considering the
benefits that the technology will bring to the pupils, teachers
and school community. If there are no benefits or the potential
returns are proportionally too small when compared to the effort
involved in implementation, then ask yourself if it is worthwhile.

> always approach the use
> of ICT objectively

A good way to keep abreast of the latest developments in educational ICT and its use in your subject area is to subscribe to
any free electronic or hard copy newsletters provided by subject
associations or national bodies. Not that I am suggesting you
have the time to read every piece of paper that arrives on the
doorstep or everything that lands in your inbox. However, in

response to our busy professional lives, most organisations will now preface their newsletters with an executive summary of the content. Scan this and then you can follow up on anything that appears relevant or interesting to your context.

 **example**

Developing the use of ICT by English specialist support staff

In her role as an English subject leader, Emma had spent a great deal of time developing her team's use of ICT to support teaching and learning. However, the focus of this ICT training had only actually focused on one element of her 'team' – the teachers. Emma had, quite rightly, invested her subject budget to purchase new hardware and software, including a number of specialised software packages intended to support pupils with spelling and other language difficulties; ensuring that the teaching staff were fully aware of how to integrate the use of this technology into their planning, teaching and assessment.

However, she had failed to consider the training needs of the support staff working alongside her team of English teachers. This was not a case of deliberate disregard, but more the result of a presumption that the ICT training would be cascaded to the support staff in much the same way as various other training sessions had been disseminated amongst colleagues in the past.

The team of support staff were a particularly strong and cohesive group who, over a number of years, had developed sufficient professional expertise and confidence to allow them to approach their line managers and colleagues with ideas and suggestions that might improve experiences for pupils. In this case, the support staff had discussed their individual training needs with their line manager, who had approached Emma in order to arrange additional support.

Upon reflection, Emma realised that during her time as English subject leader she had actually committed a very small proportion of her time to directly supporting the teaching assistants working within her team. Having spoken to a number of individuals within the support staff, it was clear that each had been trying their best with the use of ICT in their daily supporting roles with pupils. Nonetheless, they all commented on the desire for further training and Emma found their enthusiasm particularly inspiring. As such, Emma arranged a meeting with the support staff, with the intention of discussing how best to target any subsequent training.

The outcome of the meeting was impressive. Each member of the support staff could identify a number of key areas of ICT training which could potentially make them more effective in their work with individual pupils. The list of desired training was wide ranging, including:

● how to create their own resources for the interactive whiteboard;

● how to make more extensive use of MP3 recorders with children;

● the use of desktop publishing software, with a specific focus on special needs children.

Emma felt confident in the English subject knowledge required to deliver the training to the support staff but did still lack some confidence with all the necessary elements of the ICT training. This was mainly due to the differing needs to the support staff. Emma did not want to delay the training sessions whilst she developed her own ICT skills, as she was very aware that her highly skilled support staff could make an even more considerable impact in the classroom once they were fully confident with the available ICT. She took the decision to approach the training through a series of workshops.

Emma worked closely with the ICT subject leader to stage a number of workshops sessions, where they were both available to work with individual members of the support staff in order to meet their specific training needs. In practice, the sessions were incredibly successful. The presence of the ICT subject leader increased Emma's own confidence in the use of ICT and ensured that the training needs of each individual were successfully addressed.

In the weeks following the training sessions, Emma spent some of her subject leader monitoring and evaluation time tracking the use of ICT by the support staff in her team. The outcomes were remarkable. The short-term but highly personalised training received by the support staff had an impressive impact for the pupils. Emma observed support staff generating their own spelling resources using ICT, such as illustrated word banks and independent spelling skills resources. In one instance, a member of the support staff had used digital images to support a pupil in developing their sequencing skills. The support staff also felt respected as valued members of the English team.

As a result of the training sessions and the observed impact on the classrooms, Emma then worked with the ICT subject leader to develop a rolling programme of training for support staff; even producing a support staff handbook which captured the essential elements of the workshop training for future reference.

How could the use of ICT by support staff enhance your curriculum area? If you aren't sure of the potential impact then it might be worthwhile to ask the support staff themselves, seek the advice of another colleague or ask your ICT subject leader.

brilliant example

Implementing the use of a learning platform, in collaboration with children

As ICT subject leader, Ben had been asked to explore the potential implementation of the Merlin Learning Platform within his school. In essence, the learning platform provided a secure online workspace that could be used by teachers, pupils and parents to create, store and access content and learning resources. However, the school leadership team were yet to fully understand the relevance of the learning platform technology within their school. There were already well-established systems in place to link learning between home and school, as well as successful application of ICT to support teaching and learning.

▶

Ben understood that the learning platform technology could be instrumental in supporting pupils to develop their skills in the use of emerging forms of communication, such as blogs, wikis and instant messaging. He also appreciated that the learning platform provided an environment within which these skills could be developed in a contextualised but safe environment. Access would be password-controlled and users were therefore known and consistently identified whenever they interacted with the online learning environment.

However, the school leadership team had yet to experience the potential of the learning platform for themselves and found it difficult to visualise how it might be used in practice. In this vein, Ben understood that he needed to provide some practical examples of how the technology could be utilised and chose to collaborate with those best placed to provide exemplars of good practice – the pupils.

Ben approached the year group leaders within his school, seeking individual teachers who might be willing to work with him and the pupils to trial the use of the learning platform. Ben's plan was to link the trial of the learning platform to the transitional activities staged for pupils as they moved between year groups within the school. He intended to establish an online space for each year group, where they could share their thoughts about their preferred learning styles, goals for the year and express opinions about the way in which the curriculum was organised. Ben also liaised with the PSHE&C subject leader and senior members of staff in order to draw together a number of different aspects within the school.

Initially, Ben simply created a shared space within the learning platform, posing some key questions about the coming academic year, supported by video clips for stimulus and images to help engage the pupils' interest. Each pupil in the sample group was then given an individualised log-on and asked to access the learning platform if and when they had the opportunity. Some pupils chose to do so within the school day, making use of the school's ICT facilities in order to log on and share their opinions about learning and the school more broadly. Others opted to log on from home in the evenings and on weekends.

What took Ben by surprise was the level of interaction by the pupils. Using the original 'starter' questions, they had then developed their own learning focused discussions and had started to communicate their own ideas collaboratively. It was also noteworthy that many of the contributors were those pupils who may have normally been quite reserved in a classroom situation. The use of the learning platform appeared to provide these often invisible pupils with a voice, offering a means to communicate their thoughts and opinions in a form which they felt comfortable in using.

At the end of the trial period, Ben was able to present his findings to the senior leadership team which he was able to support with contextualised examples of how the technology had been used effectively with pupils. The senior staff were impressed by the level of interaction resulting from a relatively small and focused starting point; choosing to extend the implementation of the learning platform across the next academic year.

Are there aspects of your curriculum which could be enhanced through the integration of learning platform technology? Discuss the concept with your cluster colleagues and it might be the start of a new collaborative learning project.

brilliant example

Developing the use of ICT in Science

For many years, Karen's school had been investing in the development of ICT across the school. As part of this development, Karen had been purchasing a variety of different software and hardware packages to support teaching and learning in Science, as part of her subject leadership role. Her purchases were based on her own audit trails within the subject, where she had been able to identify aspects of the Science curriculum which could be more effectively taught with the support of ICT.

It was therefore disconcerting for Karen to discover, through a continuous cycle of monitoring and evaluation, that hardware such as digital microscopes and dataloggers were not being used effectively by the staff.

Upon reflection, Karen realised that this was partially due to a lack of training, as she had presumed that her colleagues were sufficiently confident in their own use of ICT to incorporate the new equipment into their daily practice.

In order to address the use of ICT resources in Science and to better support her colleagues, Karen staged a training session which would have a predominantly practical approach. She spent time reinforcing her own understanding of the various pieces of ICT equipment available to support Science and then brought these together in a single workshop. She set up a number of common Science investigations that her colleagues used across the school year and then incorporated the use of technology, such as heart rate monitors and temperature probes. The training session itself then provided her colleagues with the opportunity to experiment with the equipment in a supportive environment. All the colleagues at the workshop training session appeared to value the opportunity to make practical use of the equipment and there were more than a few 'lightbulb' moments, when teachers realised how the use of ICT could support pupils in understanding some of the more abstract scientific concepts.

It was encouraging for Karen to be able to observe the subsequent use of much of the technology shared in the workshop when she conducted further subject leader monitoring and evaluation.

What technology and software is currently 'lost' in storage for your subject area? Explore the recesses of the resources cupboard and you might be surprised what you will find!

 **brilliant** recap

The four most important messages from this chapter for the Brilliant Subject Leader are:

1   Technology can be a powerful means of enhancing teaching and learning within your subject, but you need to lead the implementation in the same manner as any other aspect of your subject with needs development.

2   Collaborate with the ICT subject leader in your school: together you could make a real difference to both your subject and the teaching of ICT skills.

3   Contextualise the use of ICT within subject-specific contexts when leading staff through a new development. It will help them to understand the purpose of the technology and the benefits it can bring.

4   Ensure your own competence and confidence with the technology before trying to lead others. This will help to secure successes which can be progressively built on in the future.

CHAPTER 10

Community cohesion

The 'school community' can mean many different things to many different people. Some people consider the school community to apply directly to those adults and children who have daily interaction with the school as an educational establishment. Others look more broadly, to encompass those individuals living in the locality surrounding the school. Taking the concept further, an increasing number of educationalists consider the school community to include national and international settings; schools which are both very similar and very different to our own.

So which definition is correct? Well, in the broadest sense, they are all equally valid and correct. However, there must be one unifying principle which binds all interpretations of school community together – individuals working cohesively to benefit the social, spiritual, moral, cultural and academic development of the children in our individual schools. Who would you include in your school community as it stands? Draw up a quick list from memory and then see how many components are linked to your subject or not!

who would you include in your school community as it stands?

This concept of community cohesion; the local school being the hub for collaboration and cooperation at local, national and international scales has been gradually developing across the UK educational establishment for more than ten years.

Initially, community cohesion was treated with some scepticism by educational professionals who considered the concept of collaborating with and, in some cases, supporting other schools and community groups in different areas as an insurmountable challenge. How could we work with a school in another part of the country, when we already find running our school on a daily basis to be a challenge in itself? This was an understandable concern for any school leader, which stemmed from the fact that the original concept of 'community cohesion' was imposed, nationally, by central government.

However, if we take a step back from the politics of the situation and reflect on the ways in which schools have traditionally interacted with the community, you will find many existing examples of good practice. For instance:

- Representatives from local and national community groups speaking to children about their work, during school assemblies or collective worship.
- Charity and fundraising events organised to support local, national and international causes.
- Volunteers from the local community working within the school.
- Class groups corresponding with their peers in other settings, often on a global scale, when linked to geographical studies.
- Local places of worship from many different faiths being used to support the RE curriculum and to support particular ceremonies.

In many cases, schools have *always* been looking to work cohesively with their communities and have many well-established practices for doing so. However, it is an element of the role of the subject leader which has often been overlooked. The job title of 'subject leader' itself could be seen to even preclude involvement with the community – you are the leader of a 'subject' after all; that 'subject' is taught within the school, within the school walls, using school resources and the expertise of the staff within the school. Surely it is the job of the headteacher or senior staff to develop the other aspects of the school, beyond the boundary fence or hedge! That is where you would be mistaken and you could be in danger of breaking our cardinal mantra: *work smarter, not harder*!

As a busy subject leader, balancing your own teaching commitment with the leadership of your colleagues, it can indeed take time to build strong and beneficial community links for your subject. However, the longer-term outcomes can support you in *working smarter, not harder* and can ultimately enrich the learning experiences of the children in our schools.

This chapter is intended to give you, as a new subject leader, some practical advice about the kinds of community links it can be useful to develop and how you might proceed with seeking out such opportunities. With this in mind, the two key questions to be answered in this chapter are:

- How can my subject/our learners benefit from links with the community?
- How can I support the community as a subject leader?

As with any developmental project, you need to approach community cohesion and its links to your subject with a degree of strategy. For example, is it more important to know the cultural customs and attitudes of children in a school at the heart of a Mongolian village or to develop an understanding of the cultural and spiritual demography of your own village, town or city? Indeed, in order to support our pupils in becoming well rounded, active citizens in the future, they need a broader understanding of the world they will be entering as adults. Nonetheless, I would initially place greater emphasis on knowing and understanding the pupils' immediate locality. Therefore, as a subject leader, you need to consider the foundations upon which you are going to build your strategy for subject-related community cohesion.

If your school has a long history of collaborating with a school on another continent, or has established a meaningful bond with another educational setting in the UK, then you may well take this as your starting point. However, if you find yourself leading English, Maths, Science or any other of the myriad of subjects in a school which has been traditionally quite insular, it may be advisable to start small. There can be great kudos to be gained for an Art subject leader, for example, taking their tiny village school and thrusting onto the world's cultural stage, by linking a whole school art project to an artisan working in the Australian outback and, indeed, this could be a stimulating and enjoyable experience for everyone involved. However, when the art project has finished, is this link sustainable or has it been lost until that module or unit of work comes to the fore again in a couple of years? Alternatively, building a meaningful bond with a local resident who has lived in the area for much of their life and attended your school as a child, could lead to long-term curricular, social and cultural benefits for many subject leaders and many different children.

> it may be advisable to start small

So, when you first ask yourself 'How can my subject/our learners benefit from links with the community?'; you need to give careful consideration to the purpose of making community links in the first instance. A meaningful interaction is easier to sustain and will be more beneficial than a one-off show piece!

In this sense, there are a small number of strategic elements which you can use as your starting points when assessing how to proceed with community cohesion and links within your subject area. (The relevance of these aspects will obviously vary according to the subject you lead.) These are:

- Are your pupils able to express their own cultural, social and moral identity, within the context of your subject?

- Are there opportunities within your subject for the pupils to share, discuss and reflect on their learning with people who may have had different experiences and hold different opinions/values to their own?

- Does your subject support pupils in exploring controversial or locally significant social, cultural and moral issues in a meaningful way?

- Is your subject enriched through experiences and opportunities for the pupils to contextualise and apply their learning beyond the confines of the classroom?

It is understandable that many subject leaders might immediately seize on certain aspects of the points above as justification that community cohesion does not apply to their subject area. For example, the DT subject leader might presume that the DT curriculum, being largely practical, has little need of interaction with local, national or global communities. However, this could be a missed opportunity. Would it not make the DT subject leader's role more rewarding and ultimately easier if the staff and children were motivated to engage more deeply with a design project, as a result of a local craftsperson or professional designer visiting the school on a regular basis to share their own skills, and to provide an example of the contextualised application of the skills being taught? A subject leader who harnesses this kind of potential in their local community to enrich the curriculum and motivate their learners is certainly *working smarter, not harder*!

I agree that the extent to which subject leaders can draw upon local, national and international links will vary from subject to subject, as only meaningful and worthwhile experiences should be sought to avoid wasting precious time and tokenism. However, with some creative thought, it is possible for all subjects to be enriched by links beyond the school walls.

How do I establish links with local, national and international communities?

So, let's assume that you can see the potential benefits to your subject area of establishing links with the community, at a range of scales. How do you go about discovering the potential links that are out there in the broader community? The key is to seek the links with a clear purpose in mind. For example, don't take

the scatter-gun approach to community cohesion that some subject leaders have pursued through generating a standard 'We'd like to link

seek the links with a clear purpose in mind

with you' letter and then bombarding individuals, community groups and businesses with soulless mail. In some instances, this approach might yield some worthwhile links, but the process will have started without any real purpose.

A more successful approach is to have a clearly defined purpose and then to seek out opportunities within local, national and global communities to support this. An MFL subject leader may wish to provide contextualised language learning within the local area, rather than being limited to the annual exchange visit or year group channel ferry trips! With this in mind, the subject leader could contact local businesses, such as restaurants who serve global cuisines or a company with European offices, seeking support and being able to coherently communicate the purpose of the link – i.e. benefitting the language learning of the children in the school through practical application. The resulting link between the school and the local community may not only enrich the learning experiences of a particular group of learners, but might also form the basis of a long-term relationship where work experience placements are offered or subject development benefits from sponsorship and the sharing of expertise from the community group or business.

Local businesses are commonly selected by subject leaders as their first focus for developing community links. However, there are other potential opportunities which are available to many, if not all, schools. These include:

- Local, national and international charities.
- Community groups.
- Local, national and international sporting associations (not just for sports links, as many now run cross-curricular educational support programmes).
- Parental experience, expertise and contacts.
- School Governor experience, expertise and contacts.
- The Schools Linking Network and other secure, online databases of links for and between schools.
- Local authority advisors (they may have experience of other schools who have had similar goals as your own, who can share their approaches to community cohesion).
- Colleges and universities.

It also worthwhile remembering that having a quick chat in the playground on a daily basis can help to build links with individuals beyond the school walls. Engendering a positive social atmosphere could lead to further educational links in the future.

brilliant tip

Remember the saying 'charity begins at home'? Well, so does community cohesion! If you are starting afresh with community links for your subject and are wondering where to start, then keep your ear to the ground. You are surrounded by a wealth of valuable information every day, in the form of the children in your school. They have many varied experiences, hobbies and interests outside of the school day; some of which you might be able to tap into to support your subject. So simply ask. Do they know of anyone you might help with a project? Are they a member of a club who might

▶

visit the school to share their talents? You might discover that a parent is a trained craftsperson with a few spare hours a week; there may be a grandparent who is a retired botanist who can help to establish the school garden; you might even find a family with relatives in a distant, exotic country who will support the study of global history and geography.

we must not forget the potent force that is *pupil voice*

So far, we have concentrated a great deal on what *you*, as the subject leader, can do to establish meaningful community links, based on *your* needs analysis in your subject area. That shouldn't be a surprise, given the nature of this book. However, when seeking out potential opportunities to support community cohesion, we must not forget the potent force that is *pupil voice*.

It is an excellent idea to use the pupils' own knowledge and experience in support of the realisation of your own plans for community links. However, have you actually asked pupils what they feel they would benefit from?

In much the same way as you would explore pupil opinion and perception of teaching, learning and assessment, it is also important to allow them to express their views on community cohesion. For example, an RE subject leader might feel it is important to invite speakers into school to broaden pupils' experience of faiths other than their own; however, the children might also be interested to hear from individuals from their own faiths but with different backgrounds or life experiences. The local vicar or imam may be a familiar face of local religious practice, but how about inviting a Christian youth worker into the school to share the impact of religion beyond the weekly Sunday service, or an individual who has recently converted to Islam who can speak about the relevance of the faith to their own life experiences?

Gathering this information does not need to be a highly formalised process. Hold a discussion in a plenary session; place a questionnaire on the school's learning platform; keep a 'suggestions box' in the classroom for the children to use (make sure they put their names on their suggestions or that you can at least identify their handwriting!). The form does not matter; it is the information you access and what you do with it which makes the difference!

What happens next?

In the early stages, it can take some time to develop worthwhile links with different community groups and local partners. Therefore, once you have established these links, it is important to nurture and maintain them. This said, it would be unreasonable to expect any subject leader to proactively cultivate the range of links that you may have been skilled enough to source in the first place. However, following our mantra of *working smarter, not harder* this is the time to look to share this responsibility with the colleagues in your team. If you have established a link with a particular group, which matches the curriculum for a particular age-phase of children within your school, then pass the responsibility for maintaining these links to the colleagues working in that particular phase. That is not to say that you should cut all ties with this aspect of your subject leadership; instead take a step back and delegate the management of this link to the colleagues, whilst you focus on the broader leadership of the subject and community cohesion.

Many of the links you will establish as a subject leader will be based on good will. Community leaders may be volunteering their time to support your subject in school, experts might be offering their skills free of charge, or companies may be donating materials to support curriculum projects. This form of support is an excellent counter-balance to the often difficult

invest your own good
will into the relationship

financial challenges faced by schools and subjects across the curriculum. However, whilst there will be no financial cost to the school when utilising these kinds of community links, it is important to invest your own good will into the relationship. For example, a simple 'thank you' card at the end of a project; a positive write-up in the school newsletter, reflecting a community group's involvement with your curriculum area; or an invitation to a school celebration/event at the end of the year can go a long way to fostering a positive attitude towards your school and you as the subject leader. This will make it all the easier when you return to these individuals and groups seeking further support in the future.

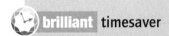 **timesaver**

One of the biggest challenges when working with the community can be organisational logistics of timetabling sessions for community groups to work alongside teachers and pupils during the school day. The result can be a constant stream of emails, telephone calls and face-to-face meetings, in order to negotiate the structure of your project. Needless to say, the school diary is a dynamic document which undergoes constant change. This can be a frustrating hurdle, as consequently you might need to go back to these groups and renegotiate dates and times.

To ensure that you are *working smarter, not harder*, once you have established the community link and discussed the founding principles of the working relationship between the group/individual, yourself and the school, then the simple organisation can be handed over. Provide your administrative staff or a delegated teacher with the contact information and names for the particular community groups you have enlisted. It will then be their responsibility to manage the logistics of visits and meetings, allowing you to focus on your subject as a whole.

We have talked a great deal about how you, in your subject leadership role, can nurture links with outside agencies, community groups and individuals to support and enhance your subject area. In addition, we should also consider the second of our key questions from the start of this chapter: 'How can I support the community as a subject leader?'

Primarily, it is important to acknowledge that in your role as a teacher and a subject leader, you are already providing the community with an excellent service: you are ensuring that the children from the local community who attend your school are receiving an excellent education, preparing them to become valuable and proactive members of the community in the future. This is your primary role and the aspect of your leadership which should take priority.

Nevertheless, the most successful examples of schools working with their communities have a simple principle at their heart: *community cohesion is a two-way street.* That is not to say that the street has an equal amount of traffic travelling in both directions. Indeed, in most cases it would appear that the community can contribute a considerable amount to the school but this must be balanced against the extensive contribution the school makes through providing high quality learning experiences. As a subject leader, there will be some opportunities to give something back to the community which will be genuinely appreciated and, again, help to nurture existing and future links. Below is a list of some approaches and techniques that can be used to 'give back' to the community in a realistic way, which should not draw you away from your primary role in the school:

- **Community licensing**: Many educational publishers now offer schools the option of purchasing a community licence. These are currently focused on software or web-based support materials for an educational resource. The concept of a community licence is that schools can pay a one-off or annual fee to grant home access to the educational product for parents and children. As a result, teachers can refer to the software or product within homework, or parents can access the resource to help them in supporting their children's learning.

- **Fundraising**: It is common for schools to hold annual fundraising events, such as school fêtes, Christmas markets or family fun days. As a positive gesture, you could approach the organising body to secure a free pass for those members of the local community who have supported you or, if they are a local business or charity, they could be offered a free stand to sell their products and raise money.

- **Sign-posting**: Increasingly, schools are becoming hubs for community development and disseminating local knowledge. If you have been working with a local organisation that needs members or might offer services that are helpful to the parents at your school, then you could 'sign-post' their services. This is not the same as actively advertising their services. Instead, they might post an information flyer on the school noticeboard or leave leaflets in the common areas around the school.

- **Family learning events**: Many schools already offer a range of ways for parents to become involved in their child's learning. However, family learning events look more broadly than just the immediate family of the children in the school. Such an event would focus on sharing the learning which routinely takes place in the school, with a broader range of representatives from the local community. These representatives might include grandparents, elder siblings, friends and neighbours from the local community. You can find out more about these kinds of event within the Brilliant Examples in this chapter.

 **example**

Enriching the Science curriculum using real scientists!

Vickie had been Science subject leader for two years and had been gradually evaluating opportunities for children across the school to broaden their experiences of Science and, in particular, to appreciate the role that Science plays in everyday life and professional careers.

Amongst the countless mailshots and advertisements that Vickie received as a subject leader, she noticed that a local university was offering a Science Adventure Day to all local schools. She immediately registered her interest with the scheme then thought nothing more of it, assuming that, as if often the case, the places at such events would be booked up in advance by previous attendees.

However, Vickie was delighted to receive an email a short while afterwards, confirming places for over 50 children. However, she also discovered that the school would have to fund transport costs to and from the event. Whilst the university was only a short distance from the school, it was too far to walk, and would require at least two coaches to transport the number of children and teachers who wanted to attend. Normally, Vickie would have approached parents to explore the possibility of shared transport in their cars. However, this set-up for a school trip often presents an organisational nightmare and Vickie did not have the time to coordinate such a high number of parents. Therefore, with the goal of *working smarter, not harder*, Vickie contacted the university to explain that she would appreciate being involved but the school lacked sufficient funds to cover transport costs. After a little negotiation, the university agreed to cover the costs and all the children were able to attend!

During the actual Science Adventure Day, the children had the opportunity to explore a vast workshop of different scientific experiences, which were run by the scientists and students from the university. The experience included making helicopters, handling live insects, creating bath-bombs   ▶

and designing the perfect paper aeroplane. At the same time, Vickie was sourcing contacts to call upon again in the future to support teaching and learning in Science back at school.

Following the event and in response to the children's enjoyment of the Science Adventure Day, Vickie then made contact with one of the senior Science lecturers at the university, who had shown an interest in visiting schools. Within a matter of weeks, the senior lecturer was able to visit the school to run a series of workshops which involved liquid nitrogen, with plenty of whizzes, pops and bangs to enthral all the children in the school and to share his interest in Science.

The combination of experiences really fuelled the children's enthusiasm for Science and, as an additional benefit, Vickie was able to coordinate the borrowing of that scientific equipment from the university which she could not afford to buy for the school, but which helped to support the teaching and learning of Science.

Are there any potential links between your subject area and departments in the local secondary school, college or university? Is there the potential for a link which will enrich not only the learning experiences for the children in your school, but also the learners in these other establishments?

In concluding this chapter, it is important to return to the core purpose of community cohesion and developing community links: the enhancement of the learning experiences for pupils. It is this principle that you must return to if you feel that the community links are pulling you away from your professional, educational focus. Building and maintaining links with the local community can provide excellent and otherwise inaccessible opportunities for the children in your school – as long as the children remain at the centre of the process.

 **brilliant** recap

The four most important messages from this chapter for the Brilliant Subject Leader are:

1 Before exploring possible community links, establish how you might like the community to support aspects of your subject; the links need to be worthwhile and meaningful, not simply tokenistic and focused on ticking the 'community cohesion' box on a self-evaluation form!

2 Use the pupils as a resource: they may well know of individuals or groups that might benefit the school through their involvement, and they will also be able to tell you what *they* think is missing from the curriculum.

3 Don't be a beast of burden – you can't carry the weight of responsibility for all the community links in your subject on your own. Once you have negotiated the terms of the community member's involvement with the school, then you can delegate organisational responsibility to the teacher who will be working with this individual or group.

4 Remember to give a little back. Nurturing good relationships and maintaining good will can have long-term benefits for you and your subject, rather than a one-off experience that will only impact on a finite number of pupils in the school.

CHAPTER 11

Preparing for an OFSTED inspection

Take a deep breath. Whether you are reading this chapter with the prospect of an OFSTED inspection in the near future, or have actually received 'the call' from the inspection team, the most important thing to do is keep the whole process in perspective.

It would be flippant to suggest that the experience doesn't carry a degree of stress with it and you will find yourself working harder than you ever have before. However, how *hard* you work during the inspection will greatly depend on how *smart* you have been, in your role of subject leader, over the previous weeks and months.

Common myths

First of all, let's dispel three commonly shared myths about the OFSTED inspection process.

1 The OFSTED inspectors will be trying to catch you out

This belief stems from the fact that OFSTED inspections are, in reality, so infrequent for most schools that a considerable amount of rumour and hearsay can develop. If your school hasn't been inspected in the past three of four years, then it is likely that it will happen soon. Headteachers and, increasingly, subject leaders are aware of this and are therefore hypersensitive to any information from colleagues about the process of inspection in other schools. This information can be helpful but also needs to be taken with the caveat that, whilst the OFSTED evaluation schedule (the framework for the inspection process) remains the same, the make-up of the inspection team is different every time. Therefore, there will always be a degree of difference due to the simple fact that the guidance is being interpreted by different lead inspectors and inspection teams.

We must also remember that as human beings we react to different people in different ways. You may well have heard of 'nightmare' inspections, where the inspection team have appeared belligerent and uncompromising. Yet, do we ever consider the way the OFSTED inspectors may have been greeted and treated by the staff within the school? Most importantly, if the school leaders are passively (or in some cases openly) hostile towards the inspection team, then this will not engender a positive relationship!

It is vital to remember that the OFSTED inspectors are present in your school to validate the school's own judgements about teaching, learning and standards. They will start with the school's self-evaluation and merely seek evidence to support this. Therefore, it would only be possible to be 'caught out' by OFSTED if, in actual fact, the subject leaders, senior leaders or school as a whole are trying to disguise an area of weakness or keep an undesirable feature of the school from prying eyes!

2 The OFSTED inspectors will interrogate me for hours!

It is common for subject leaders to feel a degree of pressure to 'know everything' about their subject in their school; in other schools in the area; in schools at a national level; and even how their subject is taught in Papua New Guinea! Again, take a deep breath! Remember that in most cases the inspection lasts only two days. Within those two days, the inspection team of two or three people will need to talk extensively to the headteacher and senior leaders, as well as observe lessons and hold discussions with children. In practice, core subject leaders are

in most cases the inspection lasts only two days

spoken to in the first instance for around 20–30 mins, with other subject leaders being approached on an individual basis, linked to the school's priorities and developments. For example, if the last OFSTED inspection highlighted required developments in RE, then the likelihood is that they will be looking closely at this subject in the next inspection and the subject leader should be prepared for this.

That is not to say that non-core subject leaders, who do not feature in the school development plan, should presume that they will never see a member of the inspection team, in a subject leadership capacity. Indeed, whilst present in the school, the inspection team may pick up on an element of any subject that they wish to explore further. For example, during discussions with pupils the children may make a comment about PE lessons which leads the inspector to look at an aspect of the subject more closely – through lesson observation and/or meeting with the leader of this subject.

The key is to be fully prepared, regardless of the position of your subject within the school. You will not be locked in a grimy room on a metal chair with a spotlight in your face for the two days of the inspection, but if you are sufficiently prepared then you will meet any subject-focused conversation with an inspector with the confidence and clarity which is required to prove that you know your subject!

3 The days leading up to the inspection will be filled with 'special' tasks to please the OFSTED inspectors

The very fact that you are reading this book suggests that you are sharply focused on your role as a subject leader and are driven to consistently provide the best for the children in your school. This is what OFSTED expect to see. Through the inspection framework, they will be looking to see whether monitoring and evaluation processes are thoroughly embedded at all levels across the school and that the outcomes of this self-evaluation are having a positive impact on the school as a whole, with the most important impact being focused on the learning experiences provided to the children. This cannot be achieved in the two 'busy' days prior to an OFSTED inspection and their extensive experience of inspecting schools across the country means that the inspection team will see straight through any veiled attempts to paper over the cracks.

To be fully prepared for an OFSTED inspection, you must first be an effective subject leader on a daily, weekly and monthly basis. Hence whilst this chapter is focused on preparing yourself for an OFSTED inspection, in actual fact, the book as a whole is a fully rounded preparation for the experience. By consistently and professionally fulfilling your role as leader of a subject within your school, you are automatically preparing yourself for the scrutiny of the inspection team. There will be aspects of your role that you will want to bring to the forefront of your mind prior to the inspection; there may well be evidence that you wish to draw together succinctly before the inspectors arrive. However, take heart from the fact that if you have fulfilled all the aspects of your role, or are at least aware of and addressing all aspects of your leadership position, you are already very well prepared for the inspection.

> you must be an effective subject leader on a daily, weekly and monthly basis

What will the OFSTED inspection focus on and how should I prepare?

A mistake unwittingly made by some school leadership teams is to forget to share as much information as possible with other staff about the inspection process. It is right that the senior leaders in the school spend considerable time developing their own knowledge and understanding of the inspection process and the self-evaluation form that all schools are expected to complete, as the bulk of the inspection scrutiny will be placed on them, in particular the headteacher. However, sharing this information and inside knowledge with other colleagues (even if not directly relevant to all the individuals) can help to remove the fear of the unknown so often associated with OFSTED. Knowing the monster's name, habits and behaviour can make it all the less scary!

It can also be helpful for all staff, including subject leaders, to be party to the content of the Pre-Inspection Briefing (PIB). This is a short document produced by the lead inspector in the days prior to the actual inspection. It is intended to summarise the initial thoughts of the inspection team in response to a telephone discussion with the headteacher and thorough scrutiny of the school's self-evaluation form (SEF). The content of the PIB very much indicates to the school which areas or issues the inspection team wish to pursue when they visit the school. However, this is not a rigid commitment, as the inspectors will respond to the evidence and experiences they access when in the school. If, in the lead up to an inspection, you have not seen the PIB, ask the headteacher if you could have a copy. It is not a weighty document and, again, can take some of the fear of the unknown out of the inspection. Make it clear to the headteacher that you wish to see a copy in order to best prepare yourself, as a subject leader; even if your subject is not directly mentioned in the PIB it will help you to feel more confident about the process. Any good headteacher will want a strong, cohesive team behind them during an inspection and he/she should be delighted that you are showing an interest.

Therefore, here are some useful insights into what the OFSTED inspectors will be looking for and how they relate to you, as a subject leader, in the core areas of the inspection: teaching and learning, standards and provision.

Teaching and learning

This is an obvious aspect of the school that will come under scrutiny during the observation, as it is the lifeblood of any school. The core purpose of a school and the driving force behind your role as a subject leader is to secure high quality teaching which results in high quality learning. However, the inspection team will look at this from different perspectives – the process of triangulation. If a number of different sources provide the same evidence then they can be confident in accepting that this is the true picture.

They will draw evidence about the quality of teaching and learning from the following.

The school's self-evaluation (SEF) document

This will have been completed and submitted to the inspection team prior to their arrival at the school. Again, this is not something which can be completed overnight. It should be a document which is embedded within the school's monitoring and evaluation processes, as it is essentially a summary of all this work at all levels across the school. You may well be asked, within the course of a school year, to provide some information to the headteacher or senior staff about your subject for the SEF. Indeed, some schools delegate responsibility for the direct input of information into the SEF by subject leaders themselves. Regardless of the degree of your involvement with the SEF as a document, it can be useful to have a copy (possibly electronic due to the considerable size) which you can read through, prior to the inspection, with a focus on the way in which standards of teaching and learning in your subject are presented.

brilliant tip

As a subject leader, you want to have all the information and judgements about your subject at your fingertips. The inspectors' main focus will be the SEF document. Make sure you have a copy of this and are fully aware of any references to your subject. It can be helpful and build your confidence if you briefly note down any mention of your subject and the evidence that you have to support this judgement. For example, if your SEF states that 'attainment for the majority of children in your subject is above average', make a bullet-pointed list of where the evidence could be sourced (i.e. named children's books; records of work scrutiny that you have conducted; the findings of evaluations about outside agencies like a LA advisor). Try to make this document no more than one side of A4, keeping it as succinct as possible. In this way you will feel fully prepared to answer any questions that the inspection team might raise, with supporting evidence that you can quickly and calmly provide to the team. The likelihood is that, as you will have already spent considerable time being a brilliant subject leader and fulfilling your role as effectively as possible, the inspection team will not require any further evidence to support your judgement and those of the school. Nevertheless, even if it serves simply to make you feel more confident about your role in the inspection, such preparation can be a powerful process.

Lesson observation

Over the past few years there has been a change to the way in which lesson observation is used and conducted during an inspection. Presently, the inspection team will aim to observe every teacher at least once, possibly returning to observe those teachers or subjects where the first observation raised a question or concern. As a subject leader, it is unlikely that you will be involved in making these observations; however, it is now standard

the inspection team will aim to observe every teacher at least once

practice for the headteacher or a senior member of staff to accompany the inspectors during their observations. This is intended to provide the school leadership team with the opportunity to express their interpretations of the lesson, based on their knowledge of the children and the teacher, whilst also allowing the inspectors to clarify whether the school leadership team can make accurate judgements about teaching and learning. As a subject leader, you must be confident that the judgements you have made following lesson observations are accurate and that these are coherently conveyed to the school leadership team, as it is these judgements (alongside any made by your more senior colleagues) that the inspectors will be seeking to validate through their own observations.

Secondary to the lesson observations, it can also be helpful to team morale to check in on colleagues in your subject area who have been observed by the inspectors. This provides an opportunity for the staff member to air their thoughts or concerns about the observation, allows you to give any necessary advice should a follow-up observation be required, and can also provide you with the opportunity to update your subject knowledge for your later conversations with the inspector. If you can provide input to your subject meeting along the lines of 'I understand you observed two good [subject] lessons today', or 'I am glad you highlighted concern over [subject aspect] in today's observations; this is what I have been doing to address this so far ...', it gives a clear indication to the inspector that you are genuinely focused on the quality of teaching and learning in your subject area.

Pupil interviews and informal discussions
During the inspection, the inspection team will also draw some evidence about teaching and learning from the children. This

may be through a formal meeting, where they ask questions intended to validate the content of the school's SEF documentation, but can also be conducted informally during lesson observations. For example, if the SEF has stated that in your subject area there has been a considerable emphasis on the use of pupil learning targets, which are understood and used by the pupils, the inspector will go to the best source of evidence for the success of this initiative – the pupils! A simple question such as 'What are your targets in [subject]?' or 'How do [subject] targets help you with your learning?' will provide the inspection team with a real-world view of your self-evaluation. Therefore, any information or judgements that you contribute to the SEF documentation must be securely and solidly based on evidence. The inspectors should allow for the inevitable 'loose cannon' in the classroom – the pupil who will always say the wrong thing, regardless of the reality of the situation. However, if a large proportion of a class give the same response, in contradiction to your judgements, then they may well pursue this as a line of further enquiry and scrutiny.

Scrutiny of work

Alongside judgements made during lesson observations, the inspectors will also triangulate any judgement of teaching and learning through the scrutiny of the work commonly produced by pupils. In the past, it was sufficient to provide the inspectors with some 'sample' pupils – often the books of those pupils who give the best indication of learning at different ability levels and often those who produced the best with consideration for their ability. In this sense, it was easy to prepare for the scrutiny of work as, in your subject leader role, you could ask each teacher to select a small number of pupils, ensure that the marking was up to date and that the books reflected current subject priorities and the job was done.

inspection teams now commonly ask for *all* children's books to be available

However, inspection teams now commonly ask for *all* children's books to be available at any given time, especially during lesson observations. For example, even though the inspector may be observing an English lesson, during the course of the observation they might also have sight of the Maths and Science books for that class.

Through this scrutiny of work, the inspection team will gain an insight into the quality of guidance and feedback provided to the pupils from the teaching staff, through their marking. In addition, they will also expect to see clear evidence that work is sufficiently differentiated to meet the learning needs of all individuals within the class.

Standards

When considering how, during the very busy and potentially challenging period of an OFSTED inspection, we can continue to *work smarter, not harder*, it is worthwhile acknowledging a benefit of the evaluation schedule followed by the inspection team. The framework that they now follow, and the associated structure of the SEF documentation, is now more cohesively linked. Rather than the previously compartmentalised inspection framework, where they considered different aspects of the school in isolation, the renewed framework now looks more holistically at the school. For example, when evidencing the quality of learning through your monitoring of pupils' work, you can simultaneously provide evidence of the quality of standards of achievement and attainment. In this sense, the following summary of the aspects that OFSTED will focus on when evaluating subject standards across the school will have many links back to the evidence used to support their judgements of teaching and learning.

When looking broadly at standards across the school, the inspection team will be seeking to clarify and validate the school's judgements of achievement and attainment, features that we have already explored in previous chapters. They will draw evidence about standards across the school and in specific subjects from the following.

Lesson observations

Whilst they will largely be focusing on the quality of teaching and learning during their observations, the inspection team will also be alert to indications of the pupils' achievement and attainment during the sessions. For example, are the pupils interacting with learning and providing responses which are in line with age-expected outcomes? Are the pupils aware of their targets, which aspects they have met and how these relate to the national curriculum levels?

As a subject leader, asking these types of questions regularly can provide a useful mirror for your colleagues, whilst also developing your own knowledge of the subject across the year. In doing so in a non-threatening, supportive manner on a regular basis, you will also be helping to prepare your colleagues and the pupils for these questions to be asked by the OFSTED inspector. This might also help to secure the types of responses you want the OFSTED inspector to hear in a meaningful way, rather than in a rushed and rehearsed manner after 'the call' has been received.

Scrutiny of work

Again, whilst using the opportunity to scrutinise work as an indication of the quality of teaching and learning in the classroom, the inspectors will also gain some information about the standards that the pupils are achieving and their attainment at key points within their school career. It is important that, as a subject leader, you have developed some contextual understanding of the pupils' attainment and achievement in your subject area, as for some children the work they produce does not reflect their level of attainment and achievement. For example, a pupil with severe special needs or family issues which impact on their schooling may not produce work which would, on it's own, present a clear and accurate picture of that pupil's educational journey. However, coupled with your knowledge of the pupil and the support they have received in your subject, the work may actually indicate to the inspectors that the standards this particular pupil is reaching are high when viewed within the context of their issues.

Pupil tracking

As we have already learnt, the degree to which pupil tracking information is available varies between subjects. Core subjects would be expected to have a considerable amount of pupil tracking and, more importantly, detailed analysis of the data which has been used to impact on standards across the school in the subject area. Leaders of other subject areas would be expected to give some indication of where pupils are in relation to national expectations, such as whether they are meeting age-related benchmarks in a subject at the end of a key stage.

If the school leadership team has successfully completed the SEF documentation, then all of this information should already have been presented to the inspection team. This means that, unless they discover evidence in the school during the inspection to counteract the statistics provided within the standards section of the SEF paperwork, they are unlikely to seek any further clarification.

don't breathe a sigh of relief just yet

However, don't breathe a sigh of relief just yet! As a subject leader, they will expect you to know this information inside out. They will again return to the process of triangulation, assuming that the content of the SEF has been generated by the headteacher and the school leadership team (even if you have directly inputted judgements into the form) and therefore seeking to validate that these judgements are also supported by you, in your leadership role. There are three key questions below that you should be prepared to answer in relation to standards, attainment and achievement:

1 How many children have made two national curriculum sub-levels of progress in your subject? (Commonly targeted at core subjects.)

2 Is there any variation between the attainment and achievement for different vulnerable groups within the subject? (Gender, ethnic minority, socio-economic.)

3 What trends are present in your subject data for the past three years?

The final question is of considerable importance. OFSTED now base many of their judgements on the profile of standards in a subject over the past three years. They have done so in an attempt to create a more rounded picture of standards within a school, rather than basing their judgements on a single year which may have had a particularly strong or weak cohort. In this sense, you need to be able to reflect how these standards have changed over the past three years. Hopefully, you will be able to present a positive picture of standards steadily improving. However, it is also vital that you acknowledge any point at which the standards have fallen and prepare a thorough review of why this happened. For example, if a drop in standards is due to a weaker cohort, then you must clearly evidence this through the use of data indicating that the majority of children may have had much lower attainment on entry to the school than is average for the catchment area.

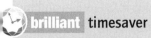 **timesaver**

In the two days leading up to the arrival of the inspection team, it is inevitable that the assessment leader or headteacher will have

▶

produced some up-to-date assessment data analysis to present the most current picture to the OFSTED inspectors, as supporting document to the information held within the SEF.

You too may also feel the need to take a current snapshot of attainment and achievement in your subject area. Well, why not work together?

Between you and your colleagues, you could negotiate who will conduct different aspects of the data analysis, rather than two or more of you all spending time crunching the same numbers to access the same summary information. At such a busy time the senior leadership team will really appreciate this focus on *working smarter, not harder* and in turn you will also be able to ensure that you have all the information you require to approach the inspection with confidence.

An added benefit is the peace of mind that this approach offers. By collaborating on the data analysis, you know that both you and your senior colleagues are going to be presenting the same statistical picture of your subject, which will strengthen the OFSTED inspectors' impression of all staff working cohesively as a supportive team.

Provision

In essence, this aspect of the inspection focuses on the extent to which the school provides for the individual needs of all learners, whether they are high achievers, special needs, fall within the remit of safeguarding, or face other challenges which may impact on their educational journey.

From a subject leader's point of view, you need to be confident that the curriculum, teaching and learning in your subject are all geared towards meeting the needs of all the pupils, supporting them to achieve their full potential in your subject. Fortunately enough, the evidence for these aspects can also be drawn from other areas that we have already explored. However, it is essential that in this aspect of the inspection, you know the children as individuals (or at

> it is essential that you know the children as individuals

least representative children from different vulnerable groups), rather than just as percentage points in the statistical data analysis. This can be effectively achieved through the use of case studies, which will be explored in more detail in the Brilliant Example at the end of this chapter.

The inspection team will draw evidence about provision across the school and in specific subjects from the following.

Lesson observations

Yet again, the essential nature of what happens in the classroom and its influence over the outcome of the inspection is evident; quite rightly so as this is what we have all signed up to do well as high performing teachers and subject leaders. In terms of provision, the inspection team will be looking at the way in which the teacher structures and supports learning in order to meet the needs of all the pupils in the class. Through your monitoring and evaluation of planning, you should already be aware of the extent of differentiation within your subject area and have taken any necessary corrective action where development has been required. This evidence is also essential following the inspectors' lesson observations as it can help to counter any misinterpretations or one-off issues during the inspection.

Regardless of how organised, well focused and professional a teacher is, we are ultimately only human! It is therefore understandable if a teacher stumbles under the considerable pressure of being observed by an OFSTED inspector and a member of the school leadership team. In such situations, it is common for teachers to react poorly and to make spur-of-the-moment, questionable decisions, which do not reflect their normally high standards. Differentiation and provision can often cause problems during OFSTED inspections, as teachers often analyse their planning to within an inch of its life, either over-complicating the lesson or missing the obvious!

If the worst should happen and the inspector questions the quality of provision in a particular class, in your subject, then your supplementary evidence of good practice, combined with their inevitable follow-up observation can help to neutralise any questions or concerns.

Provision mapping

Many schools now operate tracking systems which run in conjunction with the school's academic tracking of achievement and attainment, in order to gain a coherent picture of the individual needs of the pupils in their school and the provision that the school is implementing. In some schools, this is monitored by the Special Educational Needs Co-ordinator (SENCO), whereas some schools have involved the whole staff in contributing towards a comprehensive provision map.

some schools have involved the whole staff in contributing

Regardless of the system running in your school, as a subject leader, you should be aware of what this system is and how it relates to your subject area. For example, if you were leading PE, then what provision is in place for children with specific physical disabilities to interact with the subject at an appropriate level for their needs? The leader of DT would need to be aware of the provision in place for children with severe food allergies when involved with food technology, to ensure that they do not miss out on the learning opportunities offered in these sessions.

It is common for OFSTED inspectors to request that the school provides them with case studies of particular pupils from particular groups, which would allow them to gain an insight into how the school ensures that there is sufficient consideration of the pupil's needs in order to provide valuable and meaningful learning opportunities. If such case studies are requested for your subject area – for example, a profile of a child with severe learning needs and how they are supported to engage with an inclusive curriculum in your subject area – then you would first go to the teachers. Despite you needing to possess a comprehensive understanding of your subject, it would be unreasonable for you to be expected to know all the pupils in detail. Therefore, by collaborating with your colleagues you can work together to select those pupils who provide clear evidence of the excellent provision available to support all learners in your subject area. In addition, by working with a colleague who has a detailed knowledge of the pupil as an individual you will also be able to gain anecdotal information about the pupil. When this is shared with the OFSTED inspector in conjunction with the formalised case study paperwork, it can create a sense of the school knowing, appreciating, understanding and supporting the unique needs of all the pupils in the school.

Parental questionnaires and pupil interviews

Again, OFSTED inspectors don't rely only on the SEF paperwork. They are heavily guided by this document in the early stages of the inspection but also seek primary sources of evidence to substantiate the judgements made by the school leadership team.

It is established procedure that with the arrival of an OFSTED inspection, questionnaires are requested from all parents, and the responses are analysed within the first day of the inspection. The inspectors are duty-bound to follow up on any issues highlighted by parents and will seek to find answers to any questions they have through the inspection process. Provision is at the core of this questionnaire, seeking parents' views of whether the school meets their child's needs, whether they feel supported to help their child, and the extent to which the school prepares the child for their future life.

As a subject leader, this questionnaire does not directly relate to any particular subject; however, it does highlight the importance of community cohesion, as discussed in the previous chapter. If you, as an individual subject leader in a broader team of subject leaders across the school, can work to regularly involve parents in their child's learning, and to make them feel involved in school life, one of the benefits could be the way in which the parents present the school through their questionnaire responses – your actions as a subject leader will have effectively provided the parents with many of the answers they need in order to respond to the questionnaire in a meaningful way.

As mentioned above, the OFSTED inspectors will also readily speak to pupils at any given opportunity to gain their impression of the way in which the school supports them as learners.

At this point I feel it is essential to reiterate that the best way in which to prepare for an OFSTED inspection is by being a consistently effective and professional subject leader, who has a clear focus on raising standards and ensuring the best possible learning experiences for the children in your care. You must stay focused on the fact that you will have been *smart* in your monitoring, evaluation and leadership decisions to ensure that the *hard* work and commitment you offer, along with that of your colleagues, will ultimately benefit the teaching and learning in your subject across the school.

OFSTED will also
recognise success

OFSTED are there to inspect. They will always find areas which 'could be better if ...' but, contrary to popular belief, they will also recognise success. The key to success is to approach your subject in the same manner: if there are areas of weakness, then they must be acknowledged, and you must detail how you will take action to develop these areas. Equally, confidently celebrate areas of strength and identify the foundations of this success – most likely to be your leadership and the support of your colleagues.

That said, if you have recently taken on the role of subject leader and are now faced with an imminent OFSTED inspection, then you may find that there simply hasn't been the time or opportunity for you to complete the range of leadership tasks required of a modern subject leader. Therefore, the list below aims to highlight some of the key elements to consider in the lead-up to an inspection:

- **Know the school's data for your subject**. If you haven't had the opportunity to analyse it yourself, then meet with someone who has in order to tease out the important details.

- **Read the SEF**. Make sure you are fully aware of the judgements that have been made for your subject in this document. It is what the inspectors will work from.

- **Have evidence**. As far as you are able, have evidence to support any judgements about your subject; even if it is partially complete due to work in progress. It will show the progress you have made to date and your capacity to lead future developments.

- **Know your subject action plan**. Even if you are relatively new to the role, make sure that the action plan is meaningful to you and that you have reviewed progress with it to date. Acknowledge any time-related goals that have been missed and provide solid justification as to why this has happened. If appropriate, also ensure that you understand how this links to the broader school development plan.

- **Know the children**. At this stage, knowing the case study children well will be sufficient. If you can talk confidently about different children, from different vulnerable groups, reflecting how and why they are succeeding, then you will show that you understand the principles of effective teaching, learning and provision.

● **Look after yourself**. Working without respite prior to the inspection might feel necessary and being 'busy' might put your mind at rest to an extent. However, you need to be fresh and coherent in order to interact with the inspection team over the two days – you can't do that effectively if you are exhausted!

 **example**

Developing case studies to support school self-evaluation and OFSTED inspections

Sparrowfield Primary School had been working closely with their School Improvement Partner and cluster colleagues to develop the concept of case study children for some time. The intention was to be able to capture some exemplification of the extensive support and guidance on offer to all children within the school, in a form which showed how different types of support were combined to the benefit of the individual children.

The school then worked to develop their 'case study children'. The concept behind this was to create a single folder for selected children across the school. Within this folder would be contextual information about the child, examples of work, formalised assessments and the teacher's own reflections on the needs of the children and their progress.

Children were selected from across the school to reflect the diverse needs and backgrounds of the children, including SEN, gender, ethnicity, family background, medical needs, etc. In each case, the teacher of the individual child then started to compile a profile of the child across the academic year. Samples of work were selected which reflected key points in the child's development, and minimal annotations were added to capture the essence of the child, whilst still making it a manageable process for the teacher.

Subject leaders were also involved in the development of the case study children, as they focused some of their monitoring and evaluation activities on these specific children in their subject areas. For example, the records of pupil interview sessions that involved a case study child were added to the individual folder or relevant aspects from a lesson observation were highlighted and added to the case study document.

This continued throughout the year to form a dynamic and easily updated record of a child's social, emotional and academic progress.

When the OFSTED inspection finally arrived, all the teaching staff had to do was produce a single piece of A4 which acted as a cover sheet for the case study. This cover sheet detailed the child's specific vulnerability, age, academic levels, and any other contextual information. Each piece of supporting evidence was then detailed, in sequence, with the teacher writing a few lines to explain the context of the evidence and the reason for its inclusion in the case study. The case studies were then collated by the headteacher, who ensured that they covered a range of ages, subjects and vulnerabilities.

During the inspection, the OFSTED team performed their expected triangulation by speaking to the SENCO about the provision across the school, observing lessons during which they spoke to individual children and then reviewing the case studies. The case studies alone provided a wealth of evidence for the inspection team and proved to be a useful tool for the exemplification of the excellent provision within the school, which OFSTED praised highly in their final report.

 **brilliant** recap

The four most important messages from this chapter for the Brilliant Subject Leader are:

1 There is no short-cut to effective preparation for an OFSTED inspection – it relies on your consistent and sustained effectiveness as a subject leader.

2 Try to pre-empt the questions you might be asked or the lines of enquiry that might be followed: you can then prepare your evidence and responses.

3 The team around you is as important as ever during an inspection. Collaborate where possible in your preparations, talk to colleagues throughout and support each other.

4 Be confident in your own ability. Communicate your plans, progress, successes and next steps with clarity.

Further reading

Dix, P. *The Essential Guide to Classroom Assessment* (Longman: 2010).

Dix, P. *The Essential Guide to Taking Care of Behaviour* (Longman: 2010).

National College for Leadership of Schools and Children's Services, 'Schools, families and communities' (www.nationalcollege.org.uk).

National College for Leadership of Schools and Children's Services, 'System leadership' (www.nationalcollege.org.uk).

Tolhurst, J. *Coaching for Schools* (Longman: 2006).

Walker, L. *The Essential Guide to Lesson Planning* (Longman: 2008).

Index